GW00580141

Contents:

FLOUR POWER

The Story of the Odlum Flour Milling Families

Stephen Odlum

ISBN 978-0-9933206-1-3   Second Edition 2016

For Julie

Designed and produced by Zest Publications
www.zestcreative.ie

Introduction

In a sense this book is a continuation of a process started by earlier generations of the Odlum family. William Henry Odlum (1862-1934) of Ardmore, Bray, Co. Wicklow was the first to research the origins of the Odlum family in Ireland. Although crippled by polio in infancy and confined to a wheelchair for most of his life, he was a redoubtable character, running a sizeable farm with a herd of prize-winning Jersey dairy cows. Fortunately some research was undertaken before the disastrous fire in 1922 in the Public Records Office in the Four Courts, Dublin when so much genealogical material was destroyed. Nonetheless, the exact origins of the Odlums in Ireland, which date back to the 1640s, remain something of a mystery and require further investigation.

Significant further progress was achieved through the work of Rev. Douglas Graham whose mother, Mirabel (1882-1971) was a daughter of W.P. Odlum (1844-1922), one of the main players in the development of the Odlum milling business. Much of the material covered in the early chapters is based on his work and archive. Over time the research has been updated and an electronic database of most of the branches of the family has been completed by Brenda Dailey (née Odlum). Significantly, for a name that seemed to exist only in Ireland in the seventeenth century, it now has branches across the globe - in Australia, Canada, the Caribbean, England, New Zealand and U.S.A. - with more family members living outside Ireland than in it.

However, to date there has been no historical record completed of those family members who helped establish and develop the flour milling industry in Ireland. This is an attempt to fill that void and is based on existing archive material including a record of business and legal items notated by Rollo Odlum (1914-88) and a series of interviews with family members and other former employees who worked in the business. Never ones to seek the limelight, there are few references to the flour milling business in the printed press. What this research has confirmed is the paucity of available archive material relating to individual family members - apart from a few letters, there is little else of consequence. Perhaps this is an inevitable outcome of the diaspora that the family experienced over time, with the offspring of those who worked in the business now scattered over the globe.

What the research has revealed is the social and political environment in which the flour milling business developed in Ireland. As Protestants, Odlums enjoyed a privileged position in pre-Independence Ireland and certainly for the first number of decades in the life of the new Republic of Ireland (established in 1922), this situation continued. A view of the 1901 and the 1911 Census reveals the Church of Ireland status of the Odlum residents in their mill houses and their servants (with the odd exception of housekeeper or governess) belonging to the Roman Catholic faith.

A changed business environment was ushered in in 1932 when the Fianna Fáil political party first came to power in the Republic of Ireland. The protectionist policies of this new government brought respite from the flood of cheap imports of flour from Britain that had been a feature of the industry since the end of WWI. Both the prices for the wheat that the millers bought and the flour that was subsequently sold, were now set by the government. These were pitched at a level where the less efficient operators could survive and meant that the more efficient ones, like Odlums, could provide a good living to those working in it. With the market carved up between the participants and penalties imposed on those who exceeded their production quota, the focus shifted away from the business environment to some extent, and more to the leisure one - with more time for pursuits such as hunting, fishing and yachting. In a depressed economy such as Ireland endured for most of the period from 1930 to 1960, a little money went a long way and the milling Odlums enjoyed a comfortable lifestyle.

As the protectionist policies were gradually rolled back and greater competition ensued, the numbers of flour mills in operation in Ireland fell dramatically. However, unlike most of their competitors, Odlums were willing to invest in the mills themselves, as well as developing the brand itself. This was a feature that the Odlum millers had practiced throughout their existence and ensured the survival of the name, albeit in a different form, right up the present day.

My connection with the business goes back to my childhood, as in 1955, the year I was born, my father moved to Portarlington to run the flour mill there. We lived less than 800 metres from the mill, which was the centre of my family's business and social life. I remember the entrance with the W.P. & R. Odlum sign above it, the small reception area and the narrow wooden spiral staircase that led to the offices of my father and his cousins upstairs. That distinctive flinty smell of the flour also lingers in the memory and the chatter of the women in the packing room where, in the days prior to automation, a sizeable number were involved in the filling, sealing and boxing of the flour bags.

The ridiculous 'marriage ban' meant at that time that women had to give up their jobs when they got married, but as with most employers during the period, if you got a job with Odlums, it was generaly (unless you got married), a job for life. Family dynasties became established in the mills with a number of generations of the same family working in particular locations, such as Shorthall and Hargroves in Portarlington and Dunnes and Byrnes in Portlaoise. For the most part, there was a relaxed atmosphere within the mills. So despite many disagreements with the workforce over the years on wage rates and manning levels, the Odlums, who aspired to a sort of benevolent capitalism, were generally perceived as 'good' employers.

In writing this work, I would like to acknowledge the contributions of a number of individuals who made it possible. Of primary importance was the input of my father, Loftus Odlum, who spent a lifetime in the milling business and as the last surviving member of the 'fourth' generation of millers, provided invaluable insights into the operation of the business and the individuals who worked in it. Without his contribution, this work would have been much shorter and less interesting. I was also lucky to have been able to interview Muriel Falkiner (1895-1997) in 1990 - she was the youngest member of W.P. Odlum's family and her long life spanned three generations of the milling families. An interview with Elizabeth Richmond, now resident in Australia, provided details of life in the St. Mullins mill and the Waterford region where both her father, Ross Odlum (1883-1961) and her brother, Douglas (1911-92) lived and worked. Clare Hamilton kindly supplied information about her grandmother, Chippie Odlum (1890-1972) and her uncle, Peter Odlum (1914-83).

Thanks are also due to Alison Wear and Claudia Wainwright, granddaughters of Claude Odlum (1884-1979) whose interview with their mother, Audrey, Claude's eldest daughter gave insight into life in Leinster Grove during her youth.

Images make the story easier to tell and provide a visual background to events and people and I am grateful to Mark Odlum, Nesta Odlum, Caroline Jovicevic and Philippa Stewart-Hunter for providing photographs of family members.

A number of former employees of Odlums gave details of their experience of working in the business and the individuals they interacted with - amongst these were Niall Hanna, Gerry Conway, Brenda Costigan, David Micks and Michael Kavanagh. I am grateful to Rebecca Hayes in the Freemasons Hall, Molesworth Street, Dublin for access to the Freemason membership records and to the staff in the County Library, Portlaoise who facilitated access to the special section relating to the history of Co. Laois. Sally Wilson in the Licensing Department of the Irish Turf Club kindly provided me with details of Claude Odlum's racehorses and the races they competed in.

A major source of material for this book came from the archive of flour milling magazines that is kept by NABIM (National Association of British and Irish Millers) in their offices in London. Two U.K. publications - first *The Miller* and later *Milling* - chronicled the history of the flour milling industry from the 1870s to the 1970s. Most editions had a section devoted to the Irish mills and detailed the development of the industry in Ireland and profiled many of the individuals who worked in it. NABIM's Company Secretary, Nigel Bennett, gave me unfettered access to the archive which proved invaluable.

Norman Campion, who spent a lifetime working in the industry, has probably done more than any other individual to preserve the records of the Irish flour milling industry. It was under his auspices that many of these have now been transferred to the National Archive in Dublin and provide a useful archive for research.

I was fortunate to be able to interview Niall Higgins, former Managing Director of the Dock Milling Company, who provided an insight into how the Odlums were perceived by other members of the flour milling industry and how they interacted with them.

My thanks also to Harriet Odlum whose editing skills ensured a cogent flow to the contents of the book. This work, as written by an individual who has many personal links with those portrayed in it, must come with a certain bias. But I have tried to be objective in my analysis of the business and backed up my statements with documentary evidence, where possible. Hopefully, it gives an insight into a way of life that no longer exists and chronicles an industry which has changed out of all recognition since Henry (1802-1871), the first of the flour milling Odlums, started his operation in Portarlington in the 1820s.

A history is only as good as its source material and inevitably there are bound to be gaps. Hopefully, over time these gaps will be filled in as new information becomes available and a more complete record can be provided.

Chapter 1:

The Four Brothers

WILLIAM ODLUM
of Cloneygowan *1776 - 1846*
m. **Rebecca Kelly**
1782 - 1866

HENRY
of Cloneygowan & Kilmallogue
1802 - 1871
m. **Jane Clarke**
1807 - 1871

Anne
1804 - 1880
m. **William Hipwell**
(1st. Cousin)

Elizabeth
1805 - 1877
m. **William Henry Cleary**
to U.S.A

Margaret
b.1808
m. **James Colgan**

A. WILLIAM
of Meelick
1817 - 1881
m. **Elizabeth Drought**
1815 - 1899

Thomas
1818 - 1871
to U.S.A

RICHARD
of Clara & Newhaggard
1819 - 1889
m. **Elizabeth Youell**
1819 - 1879

MICHAEL GEORGE
of Isleworth, London
1821 - 1876
m. **Henrietta Millner**
1834 - 1873

The Four Brothers

Nearly 150 years after the arrival of the first Odlum in Ireland, the early nineteenth century witnessed a move by some family members from tenant farming into flour milling. This may have been inspired by links forged through marriage as a number of them married miller's daughters. No less than 4 brothers in one Odlum family ventured into the industry - in some instances having served an apprenticeship in their (future) father-in-law's mill.

Due to logistical restrictions imposed by power sources (most mills were still water-powered at this stage), transportation limitations and consistent availability of raw materials, a high proportion of villages and towns in Ireland in the mid- nineteenth century boasted at least one mill of some type. William Hogg's research points to the existence in 1850 of at least 3,500 mills in Ireland.[1]

First on to the stage was Henry Odlum, eldest son of William Odlum of Cloneygowan. At the time of his marriage to Jane Clarke on 18 April 1828, Henry was operating a mill in Kilmalogue, Portarlington on the banks of the river Barrow. As part of his marriage settlement,[2] Henry put up 'all Kilmalogue known as the Mill Lands (c. 23 acres) & dwelling'. This appeared to be a modest operation as it only contained a single pair of mill stones[3]. Links with other milling families are evidenced by two of the witnesses to the document - William Kelly of Meelick and Thos. Dugdale of Donaghmore, both described as 'miller(s)'. Henry had undertaken his milling training with William Kelly in Meelick - there is a reference to a stone at Meelick mills with 'H.Odlum' and the date 1822 cut into it.[4]

Kelly family

The Kelly family coincidently plays a key role in the history of the Odlum milling business and perhaps it is now worthwhile to examine the links. The connection begins with Col. Michael Kelly who was killed in the 1798 rebellion; he was buried in Coolbanagher Church - the estate church of the nearby Emo Court.[5] Among his offspring were a son,

William (the same as mentioned above) and a daughter, Rebecca. William Kelly was married to Ruth Dugdale, who one assumes he met about 1800 when completing his training at her father's milling concern. This illustrates the close family ties which marks the flour milling industry in Ireland during this period. William's sister, Rebecca was married to William Odlum who farmed lands at Cloneygowan, near Portarlington. William Kelly's first foray into business on his own, dates from 7 September 1820 when he took over William and Mary Neale's interest in the Bolting Mills at Meelick, Maryborough (later Portlaoise) which had been assigned to them by Sir Henry Parnell, later Lord Congleton (1776-1842) of Rathleague, great-uncle of Charles Stewart Parnell.

On 1st June 1827, William Kelly agreed with Sir Henry Parnell to expend the sum of £500 on Meelick Mill and dwelling house over a period of three years. The mill was to be raised by one storey and remedial works undertaken to the dwelling house. [6]

Anecdotal evidence places William and Rebecca Odlum's son, also called (A.) William, by ca. 1834 as working for his uncle, William Kelly in his flour milling business. This business expanded in the 1840s with the addition of the Maryborough (Portlaoise) mill, which dates from ca. 1827. This came about as a result of the insolvency of Thomas

Atkinson who had mortgaged the property to William Kelly in 1845 for the sum of one thousand pounds and was unable to pay his debts. The property was now assigned to William Kelly who converted it from an oatmeal mill into a flour mill with three pairs of milling stones [7].

William Kelly's own son, James H. Kelly was also working in the business, as the Valuation Office Book of 1855 places him as the owner of the Maryborough mill. But regarding the fortunes of the Odlum family, here fate intervened as James Kelly died in October 1862, followed by his father, William, in September 1865.

This marked the end of the Kelly family ownership of the business as on 5 October 1865, William Kelly's widow, Ruth, assigned their interest in the Meelick and Maryborough mills to her nephew, A. William Odlum (fig. 1). Since taking him into the business, he seems to have excelled as the Kellys developed "a natural love and affection"[8] for their nephew who had discharged his duties as Manager of the mills for a number of years diligently and faithfully. So this marked the start of a new chapter in the history of the mills, founding a dynasty that was to last for another four generations of Odlums and established what is now the current Odlums milling operation.

By contrast, the milling experience of the other brothers had a rather more chequered history. After a bright start, Henry's milling business failed to prosper. Whether the operation was too small in scale or Henry overextended himself in his financial affairs is unclear but by June 1852, Henry had sold up the mill, lands and houses to William Clarke of Rathleague and Thomas Jelly of Straboe. He returned to his farm in Clonequin but his creditors pursued him, forcing him to sell these lands. He subsequently moved to Mountmellick in 1862 where he set up business as a shopkeeper and retired to Dublin before 1868, living at 6 Usher's Island [9].

Richard and Michael Odlum

Richard and Michael (George) were the younger sons of William and Rebecca Odlum. Both brothers appear to have worked in the Clara Mills, King's County (Offaly) - possibly originally as trainees, although Richard's marriage certificate (he married Elizabeth Youell of Portarlington) of 29 November 1847, gives Clara as his place of residence.

However, by July 1853, the pair were now operating a mill in Newhaggard, just outside Trim, Co. Meath (fig. 2). This was a substantial operation with 12 pairs of milling stones in operation and as the Valuation record describes it - all the machinery was new. The mill was rented for £400 p.a. and the land for £950 p.a. and the property extended for 2 miles by 1 mile. [10]

At this juncture, Richard, Michael and John Youell (Richard's brother-in-law) were trading under the style R. & M. Odlum & Co. In September 1853, the whole property was mortgaged to the Belfast Bank. [11] The business seems to have done well during the early years of its existence;[12] but a cautionary note by the valuator of the Newhaggard mill states: 'Backwater from floods causes a loss equal to about from 2 to 3 months in the year', indicating that there were severe operational difficulties with the premises, making the mill unprofitable over the longer term. [13]

By 1862, this scenario has played out and the Belfast Bank foreclose; Richard sheds his partners in the business and is now trading as Richard Odlum & Co. [14] Now that the brothers had parted company, by 1863 Michael had moved to England and was working in Kidd's flour mill, Isleworth outside London. [15] Their business fortunes from then on were markedly different too. As Michael prospered, Richard's fortunes continued to sink and life became increasingly tough.

A letter to his son, also Richard (1854-1927), written on 14 November 1884 reveals Richard's plight at this stage:

Figure 2: Newhaggard mill, Trim, Co. Meath ca. 1910 (the main castellated section still stands)

'*McCann, Drummond, Kenny, and Owens have sent in bills but did not of course pay,*
not having any cash to do so. I thought at first, there would be a good price for the horse
(which he had tried to sell at the fair in Mullingar) *so that I could settle all and also give*
some to Whelan and Meaher; but must let them wait till better times.' [16]

By the time of his death in 1899, he was totally impecunious with nothing to leave to his son, Richard. [17]

His brother, Michael, by contrast, was more successful in business, mapping out a secure career for himself in the Manor Mills in Isleworth, living nearby in Warkworth House. Owned by the Kidd family, by 1845 this was one of the largest flour mills operating in England with two steam engines assisting the water power (it remained in operation until 1934 and was demolished in 1941). [18] It was bought from Samuel Kidd by Michael Odlum and William Podger in 1863. Michael 'had made money on the Stock Exchange and lived in a big way, driving his coach and four'. [19] A portrait of him (location now unknown) features him dressed as a Master of Foxhounds [20]. But Michael's life was also tinged with tragedy as his wife, Henrietta Millner (1834-73), a Quaker and his second cousin, died at the age of 38 and their daughter, Eugenie Elizabeth (Lizzie) (1861- 80) was only 19 when she died. Michael, himself, died young - aged 55 - in 1876. Michael's son, William Henry (1862-1934) and grandson, William Julian (1886-1973) both lived in Warkworth House and worked for a period of time in the flour mill.

Kidd's mill was to play a prominent role in the history of the Odlum milling family. It was the meeting point for William Perry Odlum (1843-1922) and Emma Podger, daughter of William Podger, who was one of the partners that owned the mill. This romance played a major role in the evolving history of the milling Odlums but this is a story that we will return to in the next chapter.

Chapter 2

Early Beginnings

A. WILLIAM ODLUM
of Meelick *1817 - 1881*
m. **Elizabeth Drought**
1815 - 1899

Michael
died young

Rebecca
1842 - 1926

WILLIAM PERRY
1844 - 1922
m. Emma Podger
1855 - 1939

Jane Elizabeth
1847 - 1899
m. **Richard Odlum**
of Mountmellick
1837 - 1915

RICHARD EDWARD
1849 - 1924
m. Jane Eleanor Hinds
1855- 1919

Mary Elizabeth
m. Irwin Turner

Anna Madeline
1851 - 1916
m. Humphrey John Hipwell
1st Cousin

Esma
1854 - 1921

Henrietta Elizabeth
1856 - ?
m. Edward James O'Brien Croker
1848 - 1921

Letitia
1858 - ?
m. George Armstrong
1847 - 1931

Margaret Augusta (Meta)
1860 - 1945
m. William Henry Odlum
1st. Cousin
1862 - 1934

Early Beginnings

By coincidence, it was the business that was forged through marriage rather than entrepreneurship, was the one that prospered. The choice of partner was sometimes a contentious issue, as the Odlums were known to be a 'strong' Protestant family. Marrying within the faith was important - which no doubt contributed to the situation where a number of cousins married each other with names such as Drought, Millner, Hipwell and even Odlum, occurring with some frequency. Nonconformists were tolerated - indeed, there were a number of marriages into Quaker families. Of these, perhaps the most notorious was the liaison of Frances Odlum (from a different branch of the family) and Joshua Goodbody. In 1758, Joshua was disowned by the Quaker Society for kidnapping Frances and trying to force her to marry him! In the end, true love won out and the couple married on 27 August 1758.[1] However, marriage to a Roman Catholic was a step too far - often leading to disownment and the prospect of emigration. It seems as if the exodus of Odlums abroad, particularly to the U.S., may have been the results of such marriages.

However, as other Odlum milling ventures faltered, in what was going to be an inevitable rationalization of the industry, the Odlum/Kelly combine went from strength to strength. On taking over the business in 1865, A. William Odlum set out on a programme of expansion and improvement. In the Maryborough mill, William enlarged the house, put in a new boiler and improved the steam engine that powered the machinery. In addition, he added three pairs of milling stones - making a total of 6 pairs - and all the necessary cleaning and dressing machinery to make it 'a first rate mill' capable of processing 450 barrels of wheat weekly. 'Fully Five thousand pounds have been expended on premises no. 1 and 2 (Maryborough mill) during the past 20 years, according to a later inventory of assets.'[2]

According to L.M. Cullen, the typical structure of these more modern mills was a building of three stories in height. Generally, the grain was stored on the top floor; this was ground and refined on the intermediate floor and the power source with the main shafting and gearing was located on the ground floor. As longer production runs were envisaged, sufficient storage space would need to be allocated for the handling of the grain. [3]

Figure 3: Meelick House before demolition: ca 1970

Having moved to the mill house at Meelick (fig. 3), in 1869, William also took on a lease from William Clarke for the Green Mills, private dwelling house and premises on the northern side of Mill Lane for the annual payment of rent of £120 (sterling) p.a.[4] The mill was situated on the Triogue river on the northern outskirts of Maryborough. Figure 4 shows the Green Mill with the 3-storey layout clearly defined.

Figure 4: Green Mill, Maryborough. Source: O'BRIEN, J. & FENNELLY, T (1996) Glimpses of Portlaoise: A Pictorial Parade - People, Places, Events. p.102. Portlaoise: Leinster Express

W.P. Odlum and Emma Podger

It was around this time that William's two sons, William Perry (W.P.)* and Richard (R.) became involved in the business as equal partners. As referred to earlier (p. 15), through his connection with his uncle, Michael George Odlum, William Perry undertook his milling training in Kidd's Mill in London. There, in 1868, he first encountered Emma Podger, daughter of William Podger (1817-1901) who was a partner in the business and later Chairman of the Board of Directors.[5] She was just 13 years old and he was 25; it was the first

*The 'Perry' possibly comes through connections with the Perry family who were millers and brewers in Ballinagore, Co. Westmeath and Rathdowney.

step in a romance that was to last for over 50 years.[6]

Although W.P. Odlum appears to have completed his term with Kidd's in London by the early 1870s and returned to Ireland, he must have stayed in contact with Emma Podger. William is reputed to have told Emma that he would wait until he was earning £1000 a year before marrying her so that he could keep her in the style that she had been accustomed to. The Podgers kept a large house and gardens in Richmond, London and Emma used to go for drives in Richmond Park in the family carriage.

Thirteen years were to elapse between William and Emma's first meeting and their wedding. This took place at All Souls Church, Langham Place, London in December 1881 - the noted English architect, John Nash, designed the church. According to Muriel Falkiner (née Odlum), the youngest of W.P. and Emma's offspring:

'It [the wedding] was distinguished by the fact that all the principal actors wept copiously throughout the ceremony - the bride and her parents, as was considered proper and natural, because they were losing a daughter; the bridegroom because his own father had died only two months before [on 16 October] and the clergyman because he wanted Miss Podger as a bride for his own son'[7] W.P. had wanted to postpone the wedding due to his father's recent death but Emma was adamant that it should go ahead, fearing the popular ditty: "The world unto an end will come, in eighteen hundred and eighty one" and she was determined not to die an old maid![8]

The honeymoon was planned for Nice on the French Riviera but as the couple set off for Victoria Station on the first leg of their journey, W.P. discovered that he had mislaid the

Figure 5: Portraits of Emma and W.P. Odlum. Courtesy of Caroline Jovicevic

tickets. As Emma later recounted, she decided that from this point onward she needed to take control of matters and this diminutive 4' 11" woman took over the direction of their lives from then on.

For Emma, it must have been something of a shock moving from cosmopolitan London, the centre of the British Empire, to Ireland - and a small, provincial town, Portarlington, at that. The couple first moved into *The Elms,* on the Main Street - a large house with a substantial garden backing on to the River Barrow, which they rented from the Stannus family. In 1893, they moved to Dublin where they rented a house on Merrion Square that belonged to Sir Edward Carson, with W.P. commuting daily by train to Portarlington. [9]

In September 1876, his brother Richard had married Jane Eleanor Hinds, a local girl, from Maryborough. Her father, Peter Hinds, has his profession listed on their marriage certificate as 'merchant' (William is described as 'miller'). [10] They set up house in 'Green Grove', a house located beside the Green Mill.

But Emma was determined to be part of the 'county' set and establish herself with a country property. She was extremely demanding and apt to throw tantrums when she didn't get her way. So by the end of 1893, they moved back from Dublin to the environs of Portarlington, this time setting up home in *Ashfield House,* a sizeable country house near Ballybrittas, some five miles from the mill in Portarlington. [11] Soon Emma was mixing with the likes of the Hon. Mrs. Skeffington-Smith of nearby *'Mount Henry'* and driving in her own phaeton. [12] This was well removed from the life experience of the family members of the Richard Odlum clan and little social contact between the two branches took place. An element of snobbery persisted - the offspring of a mere shopkeeper's daughter somehow did not seem to cut the mustard with the 'Ashfield' set. This attitude was to remain in place for a number of subsequent generations.

Perhaps, this in a sense mirrored the difference in character of the two brothers. W.P. was a quiet man, shy and reserved - more willing to countenance Emma's wishes and desires. Richard, by contrast, was more genial and talkative of the two but something of a tyrant. Known by his family as *'the Guv'nor',* he was determined that his offspring should follow his wishes and toe the line. This domineering character was to affect his relationship with a number of his children as they grew up.

Having trained as a miller, W.P. took control of the technical matters in the mill. Richard, whose expertise lay more in the financial and business areas, focused on the purchasing of wheat - the most important and costly input in the milling process. In what would now be perceived as an extremely risky strategy, he bet heavily in the futures market.

Thankfully this worked out well and the business was extremely profitable as a result - but it could also have gone horribly wrong.

Of the two, W.P. was the more politically influenced. A family anecdote recalls how as a young boy he was taken to the Heath, near Maryborough, by his governess - as a 'treat' to witness what proved to be the last public hanging for theft. When faced with this dreadful prospect, he ran away in terror and horror before the poor unfortunate victim was hauled up on the scaffold. This incident seems to have stayed with him all his life and from then he appeared to be on the side of the underdog.[13]

It made him a liberal in politics and when the Irish Land League was formed in October 1879 by Charles Parnell and Michael Davitt, he became a member. However, the movement's descent into violent disorder and the Phoenix Park murders in May 1882 (in which two members of the British ruling establishment were killed), turned him against the organization and he renounced his membership. This was not the last of his political activities as he offered himself as a candidate for County Councilor for South Portarlington in 1899. In an appeal to voters in the *Leinster Express* of 18 March 1899, he states:

'Should you elect me I need hardly tell you I will do my best for the good of the district in which I am so largely interested, as anything that will tend to the welfare and prosperity of our common country. I promise the working man to take care of his interests - he has always done his best for me.'

But he was unsuccessful in his candidacy and that probably marked the end of his political involvement, as Emma was keen for him to break his connection with Irish politics. As someone who was anxious to climb the ranks of the social orders (of the ruling elite), she wanted him to divest himself of this, as she saw it, unacceptable baggage. However, he continued to act as a magistrate, being a J.P. for Queen's County - as was Richard.

Business expansion

The first expansion of the business outside the confines of Maryborough appears to have been through the establishment of a partnership on 1st. September 1874 with A.W. Mosse & Co. at Ballyconra Mills in Ballyragget, Co. Kilkenny. From the picture (fig. 6) below, this mill was, for its time, a substantial one. Accounts for the year ending 31st. October, 1877 reveal sales of just over £40,000 for the 12 month period. Profits for the previous year reached £3,550 but despite sales for 1877 amounting to £36,128 the accounts show a loss of £315.3.0. However, a covering note from the auditors, Stokes Brothers, states:

'we think this may occur through an error in Stocktaking, the amount of the Stock being so much less than the previous year - if this be so it will rectify itself on the next Stocktaking.'[14]

Possibly the mill did not return to profits, because although the partnership was supposed to have been for a term of 10 years, it appears to have lasted for less than half this period. The mill itself was burnt down in 1885 and no trace of the buildings remains today.[15]

In 1876, William Perry and Richard took a lease on lands in that part of Portarlington known as 'Whitefields'. It was bordered on one side by the Grand Canal - this section was

Figure 6: Ballyconra Mill, Ballyragget, Co. Kilkenny (courtesy Heritage Audit of the River Nore 2009/Moyra McCarthy)

part of a spur off the main canal that ran from Monasterevin to Mountmellick. It was also close to the railway station with lines directly linking Portarlington to Dublin, Cork and Galway. Construction on a new steam powered mill on the site commenced in August 1876. A contemporary report in the *Leinster Express* describes the development by Mr. W.P. Odlum of Maryborough, a partner in this 'enterprising firm' - oddly, there is no mention of Richard as the other partner. Mr. James Lynch of Maryborough was responsible for the construction of the new mill which involved an investment of £6,000.[16]

The new mill in Portarlington appears, initially, to have processed the wheat using milling stones to grind it into flour. However, significant technological developments in Hungary were taking place within the flour milling industry. This saw the introduction of steel rollers to grind the wheat and opened the way to a more efficient means of production and a purer, 'whiter' end product. The publication of the first technical journal dedicated to milling matters - *The Miller* - founded by William Dunham in London in 1875, allowed for the dissemination of these new ideas within the British and Irish milling industries.[17]

This new technology was embraced by the more forward-looking of the Irish millers during the early 1880s, and hastened the demise of many of the smaller, less efficient operators. The English milling engineer, Harrison Carter, supplied this new machinery manufactured by E.R & F. Turner of Ipswich to the Portarlington mill in 1884-5. It is likely that the mill operated as a 'combination plant' with some combination of both the older millstones and the new reduction processes being used in tandem.[18] The Maryborough mill was converted to a roller format in September 1887.[19]

This period also coincided with the expansion of mills in the port areas of Ireland -in particular, Belfast, Dublin, Cork and Limerick. This included the new 'Model Mill' opened by Hughes in Belfast in 1877 and developments at Bolands' Ringsend Mill in Dublin which had sixty-three millstones by the end of the 1870s.[20] These port mills were also well-placed to take advantage of imported wheat, guaranteeing them access to year-round supply and less reliance on native wheats, which were of varying quality. Nevertheless, mills that had access to transport links - primarily canal and rail - had reasonable chances of surviving, particularly if they were willing to adopt the new roller technology. The Odlums mill in Portarlington was to use both canal and rail links for much of its history and the mill in Maryborough took advantage of the close proximity of the railway.

Richard appeared to base himself in Maryborough with William Perry travelling over to Portarlington each day in his pony and trap. The next element of the expansion plan involved the mill in Naas, Co. Kildare, also on the Grand Canal. In September 1878, the Hibernian Joint Stock Company (later Hibernian Bank) leased the mill to William Perry and William Stokes Pemberton for an annual rent of £250 (this was later reduced to £160 in April 1896). They established a partnership, each putting up the sum of £2,547.16 and operated under the name Messrs. Odlum and Pemberton. Originally a water-powered mill with 4 pairs of milling stones and a later steam mill with 6 pairs of stones, it produced 4 sacks (280lb.) of flour per hour. It was less than half the size of the Maryborough and Portarlington mills, each of which were producing 9 sacks per hour.[21] However, by 1885, the Naas mill had installed a Simon Complete Roller plant, bringing it up to modern standards.

This move was to prove a contentious one and opened up a legal battle between W.P. and his brother, Richard. W.P. contended that the Naas business was his own and not part of the overall partnership of W.P. & R. Odlum which had been established on 26th October 1882. In fact, all the documentation relating to the setting up of the Naas business includes only reference to W.P. and his signature.[22] Richard disagreed and the matter ended up in the courts. The courts ruled in W.P.'s favour and so the operation continued as Odlum and Pemberton.[23] The relationship between the two brothers must have been fractious with one brother established in Portarlington and the other in Maryborough and each considering their territory as their own personal fiefdom.

The final piece of the acquisition jigsaw was the purchase of the St. Mullins mill, located on the east side of the River Barrow, near Graigenamanagh - arguably one of the most scenically positioned mills in the country. The original lease held by Charles Budds from the local landowner, Arthur McMurrough Kavanagh (1831-1889) (who in spite of being born without limbs had an incredibly productive life) was assigned to William P. and Richard Odlum on 19th October 1898. [24]

Again, this was a small four sack plant, originally water powered by a mountain stream

Figure 7: Illustration of St. Mullin's mill ca. 1890, The Miller, 1 March 1948

Figure 8: The two brothers: W.P. (left) and Richard Odlum ca. 1915

flowing into the River Barrow. The water wheel was reputed to be one of the largest in the country, measuring 40 ft. in height and 12 ft. wide and remained as the power source until 1900.[25] This drove five pairs of mill stones but had been converted by 1889 into a Simon plant, using the new roller technology.[26] Perhaps indicative of the slow roll out of the rural electrification programme, the mill was not converted to electricity until 1948. The mill had good access through the Barrow navigation system which linked it southward to Waterford, some 30 miles distant and northwards via Athy to the Grand Canal at Robertstown.

W.P. and Richard were also involved in the National Association of British and Irish Millers (NABIM), a pan-island industry lobby group based in London and later in the Irish version, The Irish Flour Millers Association (IFMA) which was formed in 1902. Both attended the annual NABIM conference in 1886 which was held in Dublin[27] and W.P. travelled to London for the 1887 conference.[28] Richard was appointed to the Executive Committee of the IFMA in 1904 - the only year in which he appears to have been a member. The brothers seem to have kept their own counsel as the minutes of the meetings are strangely absent of any references to them or their business.

Death of A. William Odlum

As his sons took an increasingly active role in the business, A. William took a diminishing one, leaving them to chart a programme of expansion. He died on 16 September 1881, a wealthy man, aged 64. His will, dated 12 March 1881, stated that the value of his shareholding in the business amounted to £14,000 as well as a life insurance policy valued at £200 (equivalent of somewhere between £800,000 and £1 million in today's terms).[29]

An obituary in an October 1881 issue of *The Miller*, described his funeral as one of the largest seen in Maryborough. In typical Victorian tones, it continued:

'Every feeling was subordinated to one of deep and earnest regret at the loss the community had sustained; and the length of the sad cortège - nearly three-quarters of a mile - was a touching proof of the deceased's popularity.' [30]

Amongst the mourners, were about 120 mill employees - *'all wearing scarfs, (who) marched two deep behind the hearse.'* [31] A. William was buried in Coolbanagher church, the estate church for the nearby Emo Court, both of which were designed by the eminent architect, James Gandon.

By coincidence, of the ten surviving children that A. William and Elizabeth had produced, only two were males. As was customary in those days, the business assets were

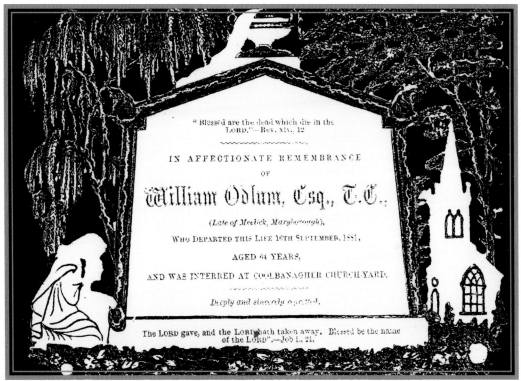

Figure 9: Funeral Notice, A. William Odlum (1817-81)

to pass to the male offspring only, so William Perry and Richard now each became effective owners of 50% of the business. In November 1882, trading commenced in the name of W.P. & R. Odlum (the sole representatives of William Kelly & Co.) when a bank account was opened in the new company name with permission to overdraw occasionally as far as £4,000 against the collateral security of the leases of their mills.[32] This concentration of the asset base between just two shareholders guaranteed a consolidation of the ownership rather than the dissipation of assets amongst a large number of shareholders who all wanted to enjoy the same lifestyle as their predecessors. This, in part, contributed to the overall longevity of the company in family ownership.

Daughters generally fared less well and were expected to marry a person of wealth who could provide them with a comfortable lifestyle. This was rarely possible especially as the prospective pool of suitors was a restricted one. In the case of A. William and Elizabeth's daughters, two of them, Anne and Margaret Augusta married their first cousins and Jane married her first cousin, once removed. At the time of A. William's death, only Jane and Anne were married and were each left the sum of five hundred pounds in his will. Rebecca, Esma, Mary Elizabeth, Letitia and Margaret Augusta were unmarried at this stage and were each left

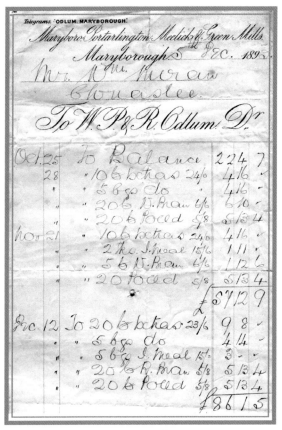

Figure 10: W.P. & R. Odlum invoice from 1893

one thousand pounds, only payable on the occasion of their marriage. For some reason, Henrietta Elizabeth was omitted from the will.[33]

As the century moved to a close, the Odlum flour milling business was now placed on a reasonably secure footing with four updated mills in operation and the two smaller mills in Maryborough - Meelick and Green - slated for closure. This was achieved against a background of rising imports of flour into Ireland, primarily from the U.S., and the contraction of one of Ireland's staple industries where output fell from 6,349,000 cwt. in 1890 to 4,043,000 cwt. in 1900.[34]

Chapter 3

A Growing Family

A. WILLIAM ODLUM
of Meelick *1817 - 1881*
m. **Elizabeth Drought**
1815 - 1899

WILLIAM PERRY
1844 - 1922

m. **Emma Harriet Podger**
1855 - 1939

Mirabel Eileen
1882 - 1971
m. **Rev. George F. Graham**

William Claude
1884 - 1979
m. **Doris Gwendoline Barnet**
1888 - 1982

Algernon Ashley
1886 - 1953
m. **Dorothy (Chippie) Eadie**
1890 - 1972

Violet Irene
1887 - 1922
m. **Rev. Frederick
Standish Smithwick**
1879 - 1962

Flora Gwendoline
1890 - 1972

Sybil
1893 - 1985
m. **Gerald R.V. Panton**

Muriel
1895 - 1997
m. **Ninian Falkiner**
1900 - 1972

RICHARD EDWARD
1849 - 1924

m. **Jane Eleanor Hinds**
1855 - 1919

Rhoda
b. & d. 1876

William Perry Jnr.
1878 - 1950
& twin Thomas
b. & d. 1878

Francis Peter
1879 - 1916
m. **Grace Evelyn Piggot**
1884 - 1973

Jane Evelyn
1881 - 1960
m. **Rev. Robert Tilson**
1871 - 1920

Llewllyn Digby
1882 - 1955
m. **Mary Edwina Bor**
1896 - 1952

Richard Rossmore
1883 - 1961
m. **Nora Gwendoline Bull**
1885 - 1950

Arthur Wellesley
1884 - 1959
m. **Olive Gwendoline Piggot**
1891 - 1984

Clara Irene
1885 - 1938
m. **Robert Ruskell**
1863 - 1945

Charles Gordon
1886 - 1887

Harold Victor
1888 - 1962

Gerald Edward
1891 - 1926

A Growing Family

Whether it was just a Victorian attitude to child bearing or the amazing fecundity of the spouses, but in a 25 year period from 1876 to 1891, a total of 19 children were born into the two families. Jane, Richard's wife, seemed to be almost constantly pregnant during this period, including a phase between 1881 and 1886, when she produced a child every year. Three children died young - one of whom, Thomas, was reputed to have been accidently dropped on his head as a newborn by the nurse.

William and Emma produced seven children in total - five daughters and two sons; Richard and Jane produced, by contrast, nine sons (two of whom died young) and three daughters (one dying as an infant). Again it is interesting to note the split in the sexes of the (living) children of the two families, as this was to have a significant impact on the direction and shareholding of the milling business. As the business was split equally between William and Richard, the next generation was to see the business devolve to two brothers on the W.P. side and the four older brothers on the Richard side. This brought with it its own tensions and divisions, compounded in part by Emma's attitude to her brother-in-law's family as being somewhat beneath her and lacking in the social graces.

Claude and Algernon Odlum

Probably at Emma's behest, both her sons, Claude and Algernon, were educated in England - in preparatory school from the age of eight, followed by Charterhouse public school for their secondary education. Both boys were accomplished sportsmen and horses featured strongly in their childhood. Claude was a good cricketer and captained his house team while at Charterhouse. The *Irish Times* of 30 July 1904 records a cricket match between Huntingdon and Geashill with Claude, Algernon and Arthur (son of Richard and Jane) all playing for the Huntingdon team. Algernon played soccer in Charterhouse and later played with a gaelic/soccer team in Portarlington who were a 'pretty tough lot'.[1]

In 1902, during the boys' time in Charterhouse, W.P.'s family had moved to *Huntingdon*. This was a more substantial house, dating from about 1800; on larger grounds, it was much closer to the mill in Portarlington. William, now in his late 50s, was finding the drive to and fro from Ballybrittas increasingly tedious and Emma was looking for an abode suitable for entertaining. The house had a large dining room opening out onto a substantial drawing room that could be used for dances. It was to be the venue for the wedding reception of W.P. and Emma's eldest child, Mirabel, who married Rev. George Graham in the nearby Lea church on 22 June 1904.

Figure 11: Algernon (L) and Claude Odlum (R) ca. 1912

Some of the land surrounding the house was quite boggy but had banks and ditches that were perfect obstacles for jumping various ponies and horses over. Hunting formed an important part of Claude and Algernon's leisure pursuits and they had their own scratch pair of hounds that were kept in the kennels attached to the house. This group was known as the 'Huntingdon Harriers' and used to hunt for their own amusement. [2]

Regular hunting was done with the Queens County Foxhounds whose Master at this time was a Mr. Knox Brown. It was not unusual for them to ride all the way to Geashill for the meet, hacking nearly 10 miles each way, followed by a full day's hunting. Their sister, Muriel, clearly recalls setting out along country lanes early in the morning on the way to these meets.[3] An illustrated address given by the members of the hunt on the occasion of his marriage describes Algernon thus:

'You have (n)ever been a "gallery" rider, but crossing about as big a line of country as there exists, not many have gone straighter with a smaller percentage of tumbles and as slight a strain on horseflesh.' [4]

Figure 12: New Park House, Maryborough ca. 1950

Both W.P and Richard lived in some style. To accommodate their ever increasing family, Richard and Jane had moved by 1883 [5] to New Park - a three-bay, two storey house in its own grounds just outside the town. The 1901 census includes three servants residing in the house - two general servants and a butler, Peter Flanagan. The same census lists the *Ashfield* residence (W.P. and Emma) as including an English governess, Hilda Ingram and two domestic servants.[6] However, the move to *Huntingdon*, seemed to require additional help in the house as the 1911 census enumerates a total of five domestic servants which comprised a cook, a parlour maid, a housemaid, kitchen maid and a nurse.[7]

Mill fires

The Odlums milling business suffered a number of setbacks due to fire - an ever-present danger in the industry- at the close of the nineteenth century and within the first decade of the subsequent one. The first one occurred in Portarlington on 28 May 1899 when a fire broke out in the screen room, caused by overheating of bearings in the machinery. A conflagration ensued, which despite the best efforts of the mill staff and inhabitants of the locality under the direction of Mr. Aldritt, consumed the mill building, reducing it to ruins within an hour and a half. Fortunately, fire-proof double doors between the mill and the stores prevented the fire from spreading to the latter where stocks of wheat and flour were stored. [8] Total losses were estimated to be of the order of £15-16,000. [9]

Rebuilding of the mill took place almost immediately and though originally planned to take six months to complete, it was 1903 before it came back into production. In a boost to increase capacity, an additional storey was added to the building. [10]

The second fire took place in the Maryborough mill on Saturday, 13 November 1909. In the early hours of the morning of the Saturday, the nuns in the local convent nearby noticed that the mill was on fire. The alarm was raised by ringing the convent bell and soon the town fire brigade was on the scene. By this time, the mill was engulfed in flames with little chance of saving it. So all efforts were directed, as in the earlier Portarlington incident, to preventing the conflagration spreading to the adjoining stores which contained large stocks of wheat and flour. In this action, the fire brigade was ably assisted by the men of the 4th Leinster Regiment, under the command of Lt. Darcy Irvine. The mill was completely destroyed along with the engine room and engineer's shop. The bill for the water used to douse the flames came to a total of 10 guineas. [11]

The cause of the fire was never established, as the mill was unoccupied at the time of the blaze.[12]

The mill was completely rebuilt by Mr. Bill Carroll, contractor, commencing 11 July 1910 and completed on 19 July 1911 when the mill recommenced operations. [13] It provided significant local employment during the reconstruction. The new mill building was divided into three sections - with the milling section, approximately 90ft. x 30ft, occupying one half and the silo granary and wheat cleaning plant in the other half. All plant and machinery was supplied by Henry Simon Ltd. of Manchester. [14]

Chapter 4:

The Third Generation

A new generation goes to work

The third generation of Odlums was now starting to take up positions within the milling business. Richard's two eldest sons, W.P(known as Willie) and Frank both joined in 1896, the former in January and the latter at the end of June. Richard (Ross) was to follow in January 1898. All three had been educated at Coleraine Academical Institute, perhaps motivated by a prevailing belief that the best education was to be achieved outside the "South" of Ireland. One can only imagine what the atmosphere was like when "the Guv'nor" was around as he was quite dismissive of his children and treated them almost like servants. This corresponds to a later incident when Frank was arranging to purchase a property and his father removed him from negotiations with the auctioneer and proceeded to conclude the deal without him.

A remarkable 3-page feature article in the 23 December 1911 edition of *Milling*, reminiscent of the current 'celebrity' magazines, paints an interesting portrait of the families. As the focus is on the newly rebuilt Maryborough mill, it highlights Richard's family and includes a photograph of him and four of the five sons who were to work in the business (fig. 13).

Figure 13: Richard Odlum and family members pictured in front of New Park ca. 1910
L/R back row: W.P. jnr, Digby, Gerald, Arthur (in riding attire), Frank; front row: Jane, Richard, Evie ?

From the article we learn that Richard, *'along with every member of the family derives pleasure from motoring, while his sons derive pleasure from hunting and shooting.'* The family motor car was a 'Porthos' - a short-lived French manufacturer of luxury vehicles. Richard farmed 400 acres, mainly used for grazing and the raising of horses.[1]

Richard seemed to be protective of his property rights as evidenced by an entry in the Petty Sessions Order Books of 10 September 1889 where he took an action against a Thomas Egan of Maryborough, who on 5th. September *'did wilfully trespass on complainant's land.'* The records show that the defendant failed to attend the court but it is not clear whether any further action was taken.

As the major shareholders with 50% of the business between them, Claude and Algernon were always going to be in pole position when it came to running the business for the next generation. Although, according to their sister, Muriel, milling was not their first choice of career as Claude wanted to be a soldier and Algernon a sailor. [2] However, events transpired that resulted in Claude being installed as manager of the mill in Naas. William Pemberton died in 1903, so W.P. snr. took over his share in the Odlum & Pemberton partnership and installed Claude, at the age of 21, as manager of the business. Like all the mills, it was run as a separate business entity and operated as Odlum & Odlum until Algernon sold it back to the newly formed W.P. & R. Odlum Ltd. in March 1935.

At this stage, W.P, now in his sixties, was starting to take a back seat and his two sons were increasingly assuming control of the business. Despite being the younger of the two, Algernon took the dominant role in running the business. More financially astute, but more reserved than his brother, he stayed in Portarlington with his father and ran the mill there.

This did not seem to rankle with Claude who, although particularly fond of his brother, felt that they could not work in close proximity to each other. He let the house adjoining the mill in Naas, Leinster Grove, to a Mr. and Mrs. Crane which proved to be his entrée to the Kildare "set", as Mrs. Crane was well connected to this group. [3] This was a bond that was to remain for the rest of his life.

The two sides of the family appeared to lead parallel lives - W.P.'s in Portarlington and later in Naas and Richard's offspring ensconced in Maryborough. In Maryborough, Frank worked as a clerk in the office and Willie concentrated on technical matters, having followed in the footsteps of other family members and completed his milling training in Kidd's mill in Isleworth. Indeed Kidd's had become something of a nursery for training members of the Odlum family - no doubt assisted by the fact that W.P. was a Director of the company.

Quite why the St. Mullins mill was purchased is unclear as the only positive asset that it possessed was its view. Its location ensured that all the wheat had to be transported a considerable distance to the mill and all the flour carted out to a distant customer base. These factors and its small size ensured that the mill was never profitable. Perhaps it was seen as a vehicle to employ some of the family members? As it transpired, having completed a number of years with a grain firm in Glasgow, in 1906 Ross was dispatched south to manage it. [4]

Meanwhile, two other sons of Richard's that worked in the business, Digby and Arthur, both went to Faraday House in London, a college that focused on electrical engineering. Electricity was going to be the new source of power worldwide and it was felt to be important for some members of the family to have expertise in this field. Digby had completed his secondary education in Campbell College in Belfast whereas Arthur appears to be the only one to have been educated in the "South", attending St. Columba's College in Dublin where he was head boy. [5] Digby did not complete the course and subsequently worked in a power station in Gateshead, near Newcastle. The Irish census for 1911 places him back in Ireland in New Park, Maryborough and lists his occupation as 'Electrical Engineer'. But, in reality, he served as chauffeur to his father, driving him to various locations as requested.

Arthur completed the course in Faraday House and although he, too, is listed in the same census as 'Electrical Engineer' and living in New Park, Maryborough, relations between father and his younger sons were increasingly strained. This came to a head in May 1913 when Arthur and his younger brother, Harold, left Ireland, sailing from Liverpool to Montreal on the White Star liner, SS Magantic. On arrival in Canada, the pair moved westwards, settling in Vancouver, British Columbia. Although Harold did travel back to Europe during WW1 to fight with the Canadian Expeditionary Forces, serving with the Duke of Connaught's Own 158th. (Overseas) Battalion, he never returned to Ireland, dying in Canada in 1962. [6]

As Ireland was going through the final steps of achieving its own independence and ushering in a new dawn of self-government, so too were there changes within the Odlum milling families. Richard's wife, Jane, who had been in poor health for some time, died in October 1919, followed by W.P. snr. in November 1922 and finally Richard himself in February 1924.

On W.P.'s death, his widow, Emma, finding *Huntingdon* too damp, moved to *Togher House* in Monasterevin, Co. Kildare. The house had been built in 1854 in the Italianate style originally for the Cassidy family, who owned a distillery in the town. By the 1920s, it was being lived in by the famous Irish tenor, Count John McCormack who sold it to Emma in 1927 when he himself moved into the nearby Moore Abbey. Emma lived there until her death in September 1939. Strangely she chose to be buried in the churchyard of St. John's Church nearby rather than with her husband in Lea Church, near *Huntingdon* outside the town of Portarlington.

A Series of Weddings

Remarkably, all the sons of Richard who married, chose brides who lived locally in Maryborough. Frank and Arthur married two sisters - Grace and Olive Pigott - whose parents were farmers in the locality and considered themselves as landed gentry.

Figure 14: Wedding of Evie Odlum and Rev. Robert Tilson - 15 April 1909
R-L: Back row: Willie, Richard, Clara, Ross, Harold, Arthur. Front Row: Digby, Jane, Evie, Robert Tilson, Frank. In front: Gerald

Ross was the first to marry in 1910. His bride was Nora Bull, whose father Richard, was Under Sheriff of Queen's County and lived in *Rockview*, on the outskirts of the town (this house was later purchased by Arthur Odlum as a company house). They then set up home in *Woodview*, the house attached to the mill in St. Mullins. Frank married Grace Pigott in 1911 - a match that was only to last for five years given Frank's untimely death in February 1916. Olive followed Arthur to Canada and they were married there in 1914. Their son Kenneth (Ken) was born there but they returned to Ireland in 1916. Finally, Digby married Mary Bor in 1918 - she was the daughter of the Bank of Ireland Manager (Agent) in the town.

Richard and Evie's eldest daughter married Rev. Robert Tilson in Maryborough in 1909.

The limitations of contemporary photographic processes may have precluded much expression on part of the subjects (pictured above) but they don't express much emotion except for the slightest look of a smile on Richard's face.

W.P.'s two sons were, arguably, more adventurous - both choosing English brides. Perhaps having been to school in England, they had a natural draw to England. Part of their social calendar involved shooting trips to England and visits to the Dublin Horse Show in August which saw a large influx of English visitors each year.

Algernon married Dorothy Chippie Eadie of Rigby Hall, Bromsgrove near Birmingham in January 1912. Chippie, the name she was known by, was the daughter of Albert Eadie (1863-1931), whose company, Eadie Manufacturing Co, manufactured pedal-activated brakes for bicycles. BSA took over the Eadie assets in 1907 and Albert subsequently became Managing Director of BSA. [8]

Figure 15: Chippie Eadie pictured ca.1912

The wedding day itself was not without incident. The reception was planned for the grounds of Rigby Hall where a large temporary reception building was erected on the lawn. A heavy fall of snow during the previous evening had caused the material of the structure to sag to such an extent that the decorations came in contact with the stoves within the tent. In the conflagration that ensued, the structure was completely destroyed as well as the 'edibles' and the tables for the guests to be seated at. The fire was eventually extinguished by the Bromsgrove Fire Brigade. Following the ceremony in the local church, where the local vicar was assisted by Revds. G.F. Graham and F.F.S. Smithwick* (who had married Algernon's sisters, Mirabel and Violet, respectively), the bridal party returned to Rigby Hall where the reception was held in the house, followed by dancing in the Assembly Rooms in Bromsgrove which had been pressed into service as a backup venue. [9]

Chippie must have been considered a 'good catch' as the Eadie family would appear to have had considerable wealth, devolved in part from the sale of their business to BSA. This might

---

* It is interesting to note the number of Church of Ireland clergymen that featured in this generation - aside from the two mentioned above, Richard's daughter, Jane Evelyn (Evie) married Rev. Robert Tilson and his son, Gerald, was a curate in Thurles. Rev. F. Smithwick also had the distinction of gaining two caps for Ireland for rugby in 1898. [11]

be measured in terms of the presents that they bestowed on the newly married couple, some of which perhaps reflected the fashions of the time. From her mother came 'an ermine coat with seal facings, a set of skunk furs, an afternoon silver tea service, an old oak linen chest and household linen.' For both bride and bridegroom, the Eadies gave 'a canteen of silver, a complete set of table glass, a collection of Baxter prints and a motor car.' Presumably this was the same car that the newlyweds set out for Switzerland on honeymoon with the bride travelling in a 'tailor-made costume of navy blue with white facings and hat of black velvet, with the top entirely covered with purple ostrich feathers.' [10]

On their return, they moved into *Kilnacourt* in Portarlington, a five bay, three-storey house dating from ca. 1790 at the end of the Station Road, about 1 km. from the mill. The grounds at the back of the house ran down to the River Barrow.

Claude, who had been best man at his brother's wedding, married Doris Barnett (who had been Chippie's bridesmaid) in Birmingham Cathedral, England in January 1913. She was the daughter of Frank Starkey Barnett (1860-1915), a stockbroker, who lived in Moseley, a suburb of Birmingham. The wedding reception for about 300 guests was held in the Grand Hotel, Birmingham after which the bride and groom left for London en route for a honeymoon in Switzerland. [12] On their return, the couple set up house in *Leinster Grove*, in Naas.

Figure 16: Leinster Grove, Naas

This pairing off and marital activity within the extended Odlum family was taking place against a background of extreme commercial pressures on the flour milling industry in Ireland. The increasing threat of cheaper imports from Britain, particularly from the nearby ports of Liverpool and Birkenhead, loomed large over the local industry that was characterized by smaller and less efficient mills.

Consolidation was also taking place within the Irish industry. The Goodbody flour milling family, whose base was in Clara, Co. Offaly, had taken over the business of J. Bannatynes & Sons in Limerick in 1894 and that of J.N. Russell, also in Limerick, in 1903. By the turn of the century, the two smaller Odlum mills in Maryborough had been closed and the remaining ones modernized and updated. Only those mills that had adopted the new methods of production had any hope of survival. Moving against this tide, a new mill was opened in 1915 in Sallins, under the Odlum and Odlum banner. This was originally established to process maize meal or corn meal under the Amaizo brand and this was produced principally as an animal feed.

Ireland was undergoing a period of political upheaval at the same time. In the main, the Odlum family seemed to have been unaffected by this turmoil. Maybe this was because the wider Odlum family was not identified with the landlord class, having been, in the main, tenant farmers and no member (with the exception of Harold in the Canadian forces) had fought on the British side in WW1. This was in contrast to the Goodbody family who had a number of family members involved in the conflict including Edgar Goodbody, who was killed in the Battle of Ypres in 1915.[13] During the Civil War period, both the Goodbody mills in Limerick suffered from looting. [14]

But there were constant reminders of how unstable the country was during the War of Independence and the later Civil War. There was an incident when Algernon failed to see a checkpoint set up by British soldiers when driving by. He did not hear the order to stop and was promptly fired upon - thankfully the shot missed. In a later incident, a group of Anti Treaty forces from the 4th. Battalion, Offaly Brigade arrived in *Huntingdon* at night to requisition a car. The car chosen, a brown coloured Ford with the registration number IK 868, was promptly commandeered and driven away. The Adjutant in charge provided Muriel Odlum with a written receipt[15] for the vehicle. As they were leaving she inquired which side they represented. When informed that they were 'Dev men', she replied that she had hoped that they were Michael Collins men - a rather dangerous, perhaps foolhardy, reply given the circumstances. Despite this, the car was returned intact a couple of weeks later with a note of thanks and an apology for having taken it in the first place.

With the new generation in place in the business, it was immediately obvious which side of the family was running the show. Algernon and Claude were the main players and their cousins had bit parts - although exact roles were not defined and job titles were rarely used. A curious management structure existed whereby a non-family member was inserted at a level between the family members and the 'men' in the mills. This was actually a carry-over from the previous generation as William Pemberton, as well as being a partner in the Naas mill with W.P. Odlum, had also been the operational manager for the Portarlington mill. This meant that the Maryborough branch of the family were effectively removed from the day-to-day running of the mills and any awkward or confrontational issues that may have arisen. How much this was due to Algernon and Claude's lack of belief in the abilities of their cousins or a genuine desire to freeze them out of running the business is unclear.

The year 1922 was an important watershed - with the foundation of the newly independent Irish Free State (Saorstát Éireann) on 6 December and the death of W.P. Odlum on 23 November of that year. W.P. Odlum's legacy had been to expand the original business - closing the small mills in Maryborough and establishing a base around the Midlands area. Under his tutelage, a significant building programme took place with new mills constructed in Portarlington and Sallins, Co. Kildare and plant and equipment updated in Maryborough, St. Mullins and Naas. These developments were to put the business on a sound footing, reasonably well placed to meet the challenges ahead.

Independence ushered in a new political environment in which the orders were changing - the focus became increasingly nationalist and Catholic. This was a significant change for a flour milling industry owned, in large measure, by Protestant or Quaker families. Anglicised names such as Pilsworth, Brown, Crosthwait, Pollexfen, Mosse and Webb marked them out as members of the Church of Ireland; Goodbody, Perry, Davis, Shaw and Shackelton were originally Quaker families although some members may have 'married out' by this stage and become Protestant. The Hallinans, although Catholic, were educated in England and some family members fought in WW1. Only two of the larger Dublin mills - Dock Milling and Bolands were controlled by Catholic families. In a sense, there was not an immediate acceptance of the new order - it was something of a more nuanced response.

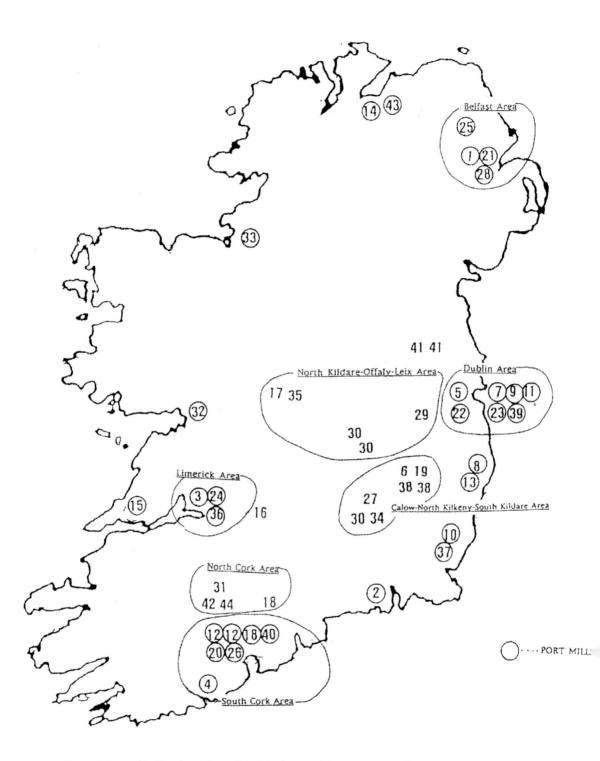

Figure 17: Geographical location of flour mills in Ireland in 1918 (Campion, 2010, p.15)
See Appendix A for guide to mills.

Chapter 5:
An Industry under Threat

I n 1920, there were 44 flour mills in operation on the island of Ireland (see fig. 14), including six in what was soon to become Northern Ireland. Most were family owned, small in scale and owed their existence, at least initially, to the availability of water power at the location. They faced considerable competition from British millers who operated larger, more modern units with better economies of scale, particularly the Ranks and Spillers mills in Liverpool and Birkenhead - well placed for access to the Irish market.

Annual production of flour in Ireland had fallen from an estimated 6,8001,000 cwt. in 1919 to 4,669,000 cwt. in 1921.[1] The Irish Flour Millers Association (IFMA), a lobby group for the industry founded in October 1902*, noted that the flour mills in the Irish Free State were operating in 1925 at 75% of their capacity. One year later, 1926, this had fallen to just 61%.[2]

New Dublin Port Mill

Despite the less than auspicious economic environment, a new 25 sack mill was planned for Dublin with Odlum family involvement. Originally mooted in 1920, construction had commenced by February 1922 and the new mill at Alexandra Road in the Dublin Port area eventually came into production in October 1924. A joint venture with other families in related industries, it was the first time that this structure was used to develop a flour mill in Ireland. Other partners included the baking interests of the Kennedy and Spicer families, together with the Hall family who specialized in grain handling and were shareholders in the adjoining Merchant's Warehousing operation. A limited company called the Dublin Port Milling Co. Ltd. was formed with a nominal capital of 150,000 shares of £1 each. The new mill was built on a 3 ½ acre site at the dockside on lands leased from the Dublin Port and Docks Board. This was reclaimed land and almost entirely sand.

The mill was erected on a solid concrete raft, reinforced with nearly 200 tonnes of one inch steel bars.[3] Both the Merchant's Warehousing and Dublin Port Mill buildings marked an interesting break with the building practices of the past. In a city where traditionally brick had

* W.P. & R. Odlum, Portarlington and Odlum & Pemberton, Naas were founding members of the organization which held its first meeting on 22 October 1902. Algernon also served the first of his terms as President during the 1921-1922 period.

Figure 18: Dublin Port Mill (on right) with adjoining Merchant's Warehouse building, Milling 14 June 1924

dominated in the construction of buildings, these were one of the first examples of buildings constructed using a steel frame with reinforced concrete walls. This marked them out as one of the first examples of Modernist architecture in Ireland. The six-storey mill building was designed by architects Charles Ashworth and Frederick Hicks and erected by the building contractors J. & W. Stewart of Dublin at a cost of £47,311.[4]

The mill was equipped with plant and machinery supplied by Henry Simon of Manchester. According to an article in *Milling* magazine written at the time of its opening, the new mill 'marks a very definite step forward in flour milling practice in Ireland, and the Dublin Port Milling Co. have a plant which has no superior in the Free State, and few equals throughout the world'.[5] Originally, the mill building had no independent grain storage facilities and was connected to the Merchant's Warehousing by an overhead bulk band conveyor. The mill was constructed in such a way that production capacity could be easily increased to sixty sacks as only one half of the building was used in the initial phase with the empty space used to store flour.[6]

The Chairman of Directors was Hugh Kennedy (1865-1936), who was the largest shareholder, and owner of Peter Kennedy Bakeries, Dublin, the largest baking concern in the country. Odlum interests were represented by Algernon Odlum and the mill was managed by Joshua Fowler (1862-1928), a veteran of the Irish flour milling industry, assisted by his son, William Fowler.

This business venture now gave Odlums access to the larger urban market of Dublin and its environs, greatly expanding the geographical reach of their operations. Although many of the other members of the IFMA were strongly lobbying the new Free State government for some element of protection for their industry, Odlums appeared to be less enthusiastic about such moves. Perhaps this was governed by a belief that their own businesses were on a stronger footing than many of their competitors, particularly as they had already embarked on a programme of upgrading and modernizing all their mills.

In fact, Odlums were slow to embrace one of the early initiatives to promote Irish manufactured products. Formed in Cork in 1903, the Irish Industrial Development Association (IIDA) was an informal grouping focused on the advancement of Irish made goods. As part of its programme, it developed in December 1906 a Trade Mark, *Déanta in Éirinn* (Made in Ireland) (see page 78). This logo could be used by members of the Association to denote products of Irish manufacture and was the first national trade mark instituted by any country in the world. [7] Members were encouraged to use the logo on their packaging and advertising material. Some of the milling families were active supporters of the scheme with members of the Shackelton, Goodbody and Pilsworth families all represented on the National Trades Mark Committee, which was established in 1906. [8] The Shackelton mills in Lucan and Carlow were early adopters of the scheme, with membership registration numbers of 2 and 3 respectively; Odlums were laggards by comparison with W.P. & R. Odlum allocated number 277 and Odlum & Odlum 539.

The new Cumann na nGaedheal government that came to power in January 1923, under W.T Cosgrave (1880-1965), essentially pursued a non-interventionist economic policy. This meant that any move by the IFMA to encourage a tariff on imported flour was unlikely to gain much traction. The first approach to the Fiscal Inquiry Committee in 1923 advocating protection as a solution to the industry's problems was rejected. Ironically, this viewpoint was not shared by the IIDA who felt that it would alienate their Trade Mark users in Ireland. [9]

Conditions within the industry continued to deteriorate with a number of mills closing down, including the Hallinan operation in Fermoy in 1926. The IFMA continued to lobby for protection of the local industry advocating to the Tariff Commission in March 1927 for the imposition of a tariff of 3/- per sack on imported flour. But this was also rejected. There was a sense that the IFMA were not presenting a united front - those supporting protectionism tended to be from the less profitable operators in the most severely depressed milling regions - Shackeltons in Carlow, Goodbodys in Limerick and Clara and Furlongs in Cork. [10] The Dublin Port Milling Co. and Bolands were less enthusiastic - their modern, highly capitalized facilities were more likely to be able to withstand the threat posed by English flour imports from mills owned by Ranks and Spillers who had built up a considerable trade in Ireland.

Ranks come to Ireland

In fact, it was one of those English millers that was now to have a fundamental impact on the structure of the industry, the way it operated and indeed, the way in which the milling families lived their lives. Ranks and Spillers had both, naturally, opposed the imposition of any tariff. But it was Ranks, perhaps sensing that tariffs were inevitable and aware of the weakness of the native industry, who seized the initiative. Clandestine negotiations between Goodbodys and Ranks commenced in 1929 - the Goodbody businesses were in a parlous state, undercapitalized and paying out large dividends to fund a generous lifestyle for a large number of family members.[11] A deal was concluded and publicly announced on 25 February 1930 with Ranks taking over Bannatynes in Limerick, its two subsidiary companies and M.J. & L. Goodbody in Clara. [12] At the same time, Spillers attempted to gain a foothold in the Irish market through the purchase of the Dublin Port Mill but their approach to the shareholders was rebuffed. [13]

At a single stroke, Ranks had now secured a 30% market share of the Irish flour market. It was a somewhat incongruous turn of events whereby an English company, within eight years of the country achieving its own independence, acquired what many perceived as a vital local industry.

Initially suspicious of the arrival of such a powerful competitor in their midst, the other millers soon warmed to the idea. This can be gauged from an extract from the report from the AGM of the IFMA which was held on 4th. December 1930 which stated:

'The most important event of the year was the purchase of interest in the largest Milling concern in the Irish Free State. Although fears were expressed, especially by outsiders, that the results would be detrimental to the Irish Flour Milling Trade, the experience of our members has been that on the whole the change resulted in stabilizing prices and a general improvement in business methods of the whole trade.' [14]

With a foot firmly based in both camps, Ranks were able to broker a deal between the newly formed Flour Millers' Economic Association in Ireland and the English Mutual Millers' Association. A market-sharing agreement in 1931 between the two groups effectively established a cartel within the industry. The market was carved up between the Irish and British millers with quotas allocated to each group based on market shares that had prevailed in the years 1926-27. This effectively gave the Irish millers a higher share than had existed in 1930. [15]

Faced with what was essentially a controlled market, the Cumann nGaedheal government chose to do nothing, by their inaction tacitly agreeing to the protection of the flour milling industry. Although some mills had closed in the interim, falling from a total of 44 in 1918 to just

28 in 1932 (the final year of the Cumann nGaedheal government), many of the surviving mills were still too small and inefficient to be economically viable in the longer term.

However, significant changes in economic policy emerged with a change of government. In March 1932 the Fianna Fáil government under de Valera came to power for the first time. It chose instead an active policy of protectionism, moving Ireland from a relatively open economy to one of the most protected in Europe. This policy was to have a profound impact on the flour milling industry, effectively changing it from an industry sponsored cartel to essentially a state sponsored one. After many years of contraction, the next decade was to witness a new level of expansion with the construction of a number of new mills around the country. Some of these were built more on the basis of political considerations rather than economic ones and were unlikely to prosper. However, for the next decade or so, the flour milling industry was to witness a level of prosperity that it had rarely reached before.

Figure 19: A group of Odlum employees from Portlaoise Mill : 1936
Back row: Peter O'Brien, Danny Marum, Jack Flanagan, James McEvoy, Tom Dunne
Third row: Willie Guilfoyle, James O'Brien, Jack Lalor, Jack Whelan, Steven Brennan, James Ging, Paddy McEvoy. Second Row:
Matt Brophy, Sam Lowe, Jack Guilfoyle, Willie Garret, Michael McEvoy, Gerry Dunne, Mick Kavanagh. Front: Paddy Doran, Jack
Dunne, Paddy O'Brien, Bill Moran
Source: O'BRIEN, J. (2013) As times go by - photographs and memories. Arderin Publishing Company. (p. 56)

Chapter 6:
An Improving Landscape

The new Fianna Fáil government embarked on a policy of economic self-sufficiency that was pursued with a missionary zeal. Out went all notions of free trade, *laissez faire* and support for cattle based agriculture. In came protectionism and a new focus on tillage, particularly wheat growing and support for the smaller farmers who were the bedrock of support for Fianna Fáil. [1]

Protectionism

The Irish millers themselves had no input into this change in policy, especially as they saw no need to change the existing deal with the Mutual Millers' Association. However, the new Minister for Industry and Commerce, Sean Lemass, was suspicious of the English-owned Ranks' intentions and was keen to reduce their influence in the Irish market. To provide an outlet for the increased acreage under wheat that must now be converted into flour, the government introduced a significant measure of protectionism into the market. Through the FINANCE (CUSTOMS DUTIES)(NO. 3) ACT, 1932, which came into effect on 1 September, a tariff of 5/- per sack - 2/- more than the millers had sought in 1927 (see p. 43)- was imposed on all flour and wheatmeal. [2] As a direct consequence, the export of flour from Northern Ireland to the Republic was effectively barred. This posed serious problems for Northern millers, such as Andrews, as at least half of their total output was sold south of the border, particularly in Co. Donegal. [3]

The new government also took steps to regulate the flour milling industry through the AGRICULTURAL PRODUCE (CEREALS) ACT, 1933. This established a licensing system under which only approved mills could produce flour. As well as setting an output quota of flour for each miller, it also stipulated a minimum quantity of home produced wheat that had to be used by the home based millers. [4] The State effectively took control of the industry as the Minister for Industry and Commerce now had the power to grant, refuse or revoke licenses.

As a result of the restrictions placed on the import of flour, the quantities shipped into the country fell sharply from 3,377,092 cwt. in 1931 to just 227,951 cwt. in 1935. [5] Importers of flour (mainly Spillers through the Higgins family in Cork) were effectively put out of business and their claims for compensation from the government fell on deaf ears.

The reduction in imports opened up the opportunity for the Irish based mills to expand production and this saw a corresponding increase in output. Flour production in the Free State rose from 3,930,852 cwt. in 1932 to 6,804,113 cwt. in 1936 with the numbers of mills operating rising from 28 to 37 over the same period.[6] This additional capacity arose through a combination of newly built mills (Cork, Waterford, Ballina, and Milford, Co. Donegal), the reopening of previously closed mills (Carlow, Wicklow and Dock Mill in Dublin) and increased capacity (the Dublin Port Mill, where the mill was doubled in size).

The Odlum family was involved in a number of these developments. In the Dublin Port Mill production capacity was added and new wheat storage capacity built on the site in 1935. In Waterford, a licence was granted for a new flour mill in 1933 despite a strong protest from a meeting of representatives of mill workers in the neighbouring counties of Carlow, Tipperary, Wexford and Kilkenny.[7]

Waterford Flour Mills Ltd. was incorporated in 1933 with a share capital of £15,000, later increased to £120,000. Both Algernon and Claude Odlum were directors of the company along with Sir Henry James Forde and T.W.H. Davies.[8] It was built on a riverside site at Ferrybank, across the river from the city. Before the foundations were laid the first of 300 piles, 38ft. long, was sunk on 4 January 1934. Erection of the mill proper commenced in March by the contractors, Peter Lind & Co. of London and the building was completed by the end of the year.[9]

Figure 20: Sean Lemass (R) pictured at opening of National Flour Mills, Cork in 1934

Figure 21: Dublin Port Mill - new wheat silo - September 1935 Note how all the workmen seem to be posing for the camera!

Algernon had also become more involved on the political stage. He had already been asked by the previous Cumann na nGadhael government in 1929 to be part of a three member Court of inquiry to investigate the causes and circumstances of the Dublin Tramway dispute which had left the city without trams for three weeks.[10] In 1933, he was appointed by the Minister for Industry and Commerce, Sean Lemass, as one of the members of the Milling Advisory Committee set up under the AGRICULTURAL PRODUCE (CEREALS) ACT to assist the Minister on milling issues.[11] Indeed, despite their widely differing backgrounds, Algernon enjoyed a good relationship with Lemass.

The new licencing system worked to the advantage of the larger, more efficient mills. The price of flour was pitched at a level that allowed the smaller, inland mills to make a profit, ensuring bumper returns for the larger operators.[12] Prices rose significantly - from 10s. 4d. per cwt. in 1934 to 12s. 7d. in 1935 - amid rumblings of discontent at the political level.[13] But Fianna

Fáil remained resolute in their policies despite their questionable economic and financial bases. In the drive towards economic self-sufficiency, the acreage under wheat grew substantially, from just over 21,000 acres in 1932 to over 254,000 acres in 1936.[14] This brought its own set of problems for the millers as this glut in supply necessitated the construction of additional storage space for a raw material that was often borderline in terms of suitability for the production of flour.

The new mills opened up in places such as Milford in Donegal and Ballina, Co. Mayo were built with more emphasis on job creation than sound monetary principles. Far removed from supplies of raw materials and customers for their end product, they were operating under a handicap from day one.

Nevertheless, increases in the price of flour were accepted by the government as a trade-off for the ever increasing amounts of native wheat used by the millers and the cost of keeping less efficient mills in operation. As conditions within the industry improved, so too did the prospects of those working in it. Total numbers employed in the industry rose from a total of 1,979 in 1931 to 2,739 in 1936.[15] At a time when wage rates within Irish industry were generally stagnating, those in the flour milling industry actually increased.

The quota system and the effective cartel that this introduced removed, in essence, all elements of competition within the industry and stifled innovation. It ultimately postponed the rationalization of the industry for another 20 years. As there were penalties for exceeding the quota allocated to each mill, there was no sense in pushing for additional business, so an atmosphere of inertia prevailed. As the Odlums were making a comfortable living out of the business and there were a series of General Managers in place to run the various operations, there was more time to indulge themselves in their outside interests. In addition, Algernon and Claude Odlum were running the show and they did not want their cousins interfering in the operation of the mills. This effectively ruled them out of the day-to-day elements of the business.

Richard Odlum's sons

Richard's son, Ross * Odlum, moved from St. Mullins in 1926 to take up residence in *Sion Hill*, in Waterford city. This was a substantial property on about 7 acres in Ferrybank, near the mill. Employed in the upkeep were a parlour maid, a house maid, cook and two men outside, one who looked after the garden and the other the horses. The gardener had been trained in the Botanic Gardens in Dublin and produced many prize winning exhibits that were entered into local shows. Along with azaleas and rhododendrons, there were a number of specimen trees on the property, including a large tulip tree (only identified on the basis of a photograph sent to *Country Life* magazine), most of which have since succumbed to the ravages of time. [16]

*He was actually christened Richard Edward but a subsequent visit to Maryborough by Lord Rossmore inspired his father to name him Rossmore - (normally abbreviated to 'Ross').

Quite why Ross moved to Waterford is unclear as he was to have no input into the running of the mill there. Perhaps the family found the isolation of St. Mullin's too much to bear and wanted to be part of larger centre of population where there was more activity. As his was a musical family and Waterford had a thriving amateur musical scene, perhaps this was the draw. Ross's wife, Nora, who was a very sociable person and had a fine voice, used to accompany the well known Irish tenor, Willie Watt, at recitals and concerts that were given in the area. [17]

The family enjoyed an active social life with lots of music and tea parties - included in their circle of friends were members of the hunt, fellow parishioners of the local parish church [18] and personnel from the local Bank of Ireland.

During the Troubles, Ross had to endure a frightening incident at the mill in St. Mullin's. A group of armed IRA men came into the mill and ordered Ross into the mill office. Whatever their intentions, they were never made clear as just as this was happening, the mill engine backfired, producing a sound like an explosion. Thinking that the Black and Tans were now on the scene, the rebels fled, leaving Ross none the worse for the incident. [19]

Like many of the other family members, Ross had a passion for horses and hunting. He worked in St. Mullin's three days a week and hunted the other two. There were three packs of hounds in the area - the Waterford Foxhounds, the Kilkenny Foxhounds and the Gaultier Harriers. He continued to hunt until 1945, retiring at the age of 62. [20] Sports featured large in the life of the family - fishing was a favourite pastime as was golf, with a course accessible immediately behind the house in Ferrybank. Something of a routine emerged whereby after Sunday lunch, Ross would play with Harry White, whose son (also Harry) worked in the flour mill in Waterford. Ross and Nora used to take holidays each year in June in the Butler Arms Hotel in Waterville, Co. Kerry for the angling and golf.[21] During the summer months, Ross lived during the week in a hut that he built in the woods above the river in St. Mullin's, returning to Waterford for the weekend.

As part of a series on local personalities, Ross featured in the 19 April 1946 edition of the *Munster Express* newspaper. The text that accompanied the cartoon perhaps best summed up the individual:

'*One of Waterford's most genial businessmen, and Grand Old Man of the Hunting Field. Still thrills to the Huntsman's horn of the Waterford and Gaultier Hounds. Yet an active member of Waterford Golf Club whilst he sights a double barrel and casts a fly with the true sportsman's eye. Affable, agreeable and though affluent, is devoid of affectation. And for all his milling prowess, knows nothing of the milling ways of life.*'

Ross was also a regular attendee at the National Association of British and Irish Millers' annual convention in England, representing Odlums in 1932 and 1933. This became something

Figure 22: Ross Odlum. - Munster Express, 19 April 1946

of a marriage bureau for the family as his daughter, Sheila met her future husband, Harold Thomas, at one of the gatherings as did his son, Douglas - although in his instance his future wife was staying in the convention hotel rather than being part of the milling fraternity. These conventions were very sociable events with a number of sporting events and cultural visits laid on for the participants. The Odlums excelled in the tennis events, being winners of the doubles on a number of occasions - Algy in 1936 and Cyril (see p. 62) in 1948.

Willie never married, although there was a story that he took a shining to the new housekeeper, a Miss Peacock, who came to New Park to manage the house on his mother's death. However, this liaison was never going to advance as his father was quick to dispel any notions of a possible match. Whether it was in response to this is unknown, but Willie became an inveterate traveller. Records show him travelling in 1920 to Kingstown, Jamaica with his uncle, W.P. Odlum, who was then 75; once to South Africa in 1932 and three times to Buenos Aires, Argentina in 1930, 1935 and 1937. He also embarked on what was something of a round-the-world adventure, leaving Quebec for Queenstown, New Zealand on 15 June 1925 and returning almost eight months later on 13 February 1926 from Colombo accompanied, by this stage, by his younger brother, Gerald. On some of the trips he was accompanied by his nephews, Robert Roland (Rollo) Odlum and Cecil Tilson (both of whose fathers had died young) with the former going on both of the later trips to Buenos Aires and the latter to Cape Town in 1932.[22]

Officially the miller in Portlaoise*, but with a non-family member in place as General Manager (Albert McClure and latterly Lewis (Lew) Sharpe), Willie's work regime appeared to be quite flexible which allowed him considerable time off to do his travelling. Absences of over a month were not uncommon.

Digby, who was always frail, was afflicted by the Spanish flu pandemic that swept Europe in 1918-9. This left him weakened and unable to work on a consistent basis.

*Maryborough had been renamed Portlaoise post Independence but family members continued to refer to it by its previous name right up to the end of 1960s. The name of the mill is only changed in 1962 in the list of members of IFMA, from Maryborough to Portlaoighise (sic).

Figure 23: NABIM Convention groups: Bottom: Bournemouth June 1933: (l/r) H.K. Frost, Sheila Odlum, Chippie Odlum. Top: Turnberry, June 1934: (l/r) J.V. Rank, C. Neil, Claude Odlum, Doris Odlum. Source: Milling

Apart from taking the odd moisture test on wheat prior to milling, his was a watching brief - 'keeping an eye on things'. He epitomized a common description used for people of his type - 'a lovely man' - a gentleman of manners but no particular ambition.

Of the four sons of Richard's who were now involved in the business, Arthur was the most capable. He was active in the Freemasons of Ireland for most of his working life, joining the Maryborough Lodge No. 398 in 1913 (Willie and Ross were also Freemasons). Arthur worked his way up the ranks over the years, finally becoming Provincial Grand Master of the Midland Counties in 1943, a position he held until he retired from the post in 1955. [23] Arthur also was a committee member of the IFMA from 1934-7, serving as Vice President in 1936.

Arthur's membership of the Freemasons engendered a spirit of good works and this manifested itself in a rather strange ritual, perhaps more indicative of the levels of poverty in Portlaoise than Arthur's generosity. On Friday afternoons, Arthur used to stand outside the mill office in Portlaoise and throw out the coins from his pockets to a crowd that had gathered outside.

The year 1935 marked a change of residence for a number of the Portlaoise families. Willie moved out of *New Park* to take up residence in *Graigaverne* on the Dublin Road outside Ballybrittas, Co. Laois. Willie's place in *New Park* was taken by Evie (Rev. Robert Tilson's widow), who remarried in 1930 to Lew Sharpe.

Digby, who had unofficially 'retired' at this stage, left *Meelick House* and moved to Dublin,

Figure 24: Family Group (l-r) Ross, Arthur, Willie, Douglas ca 1950.

renting a house, *Druid Hill* in Killiney, Co. Dublin. This afforded his wife, Mary, a temporary respite from family tensions in Portlaoise, and she revelled in the new social and cultural opportunities that the capital city offered.

With the deaths of W.P. snr. and Richard, the business had passed on to the next generation. A new partnership was formed on 15 December 1925 with the same 50:50 split between the two sides of the family. However, with an increasing number of sons involved in the business, this resulted in Algernon and Claude each having a 25% share in the business and a four way split on the other side with Ross, Digby, Willie and Arthur each with 12.5% of the business.[24] There was a suggestion that Digby's three brothers tried to force him out at this stage but that his wife, Mary, saved the day by going along to a Board meeting and hammering on the table to protest and argue Digby's case!

Claude and Algernon Odlum

But it was obvious where the power lay. Algernon and Claude were the main movers and the ones who represented the family's interest in the IFMA. Claude acted as the organisation's Treasurer and Secretary from 1917 to 1941 and was on the Exececutive Committee from 1950 to 1954. Algernon served as President on 3 occasions. The first of these was in 1921-2, followed by consecutive terms from 1939 to 1941, during which he steered the industry through the difficult early war years when supplies of raw materials, particularly wheat, were tight.

Claude was a Director of the Bank of Ireland from 1929-1966 and acted as Governor for a period of two years 1943-5. He was also a Director of the Grand Canal Co. (as was his father, W.P.) from 1927 up to the time of its dissolution in May 1950. Frugal in his lifestyle, he preferred to spend his money on bloodstock, owning a series of racehorses. Although both his father and brother were occasional owners of racehorses, Claude had a long association with the sport from the early years with aptly named 'War Flour' who won the 2 mile Hill Chase at Bellewstown Races in 1917 [25], right up to 'Wily Trout' in 1965 (see Appendix B for a complete record of his racehorses). His racing colours were claret jacket with claret and white quartered cap.

An article in the *Irish Times* from 12 April 1927 featuring his 'Tony Boy', who was a winner in the Lough Ennel Plate in Mullingar, described Claude as follows: 'Mr. Odlum has only a few horses in training but manages to pick up a race now and then, and is the stamp of a owner one likes to see successful.'

Claude had a long association with the Kildare Hunt and rode in the inaugural Naas Harriers point-to-point in March 1920. Ironically, Doris, his wife, hated horses and never really settled into the Irish way of life. Claude and Doris had four children, Tony, Audrey, Corinne and Mavis. Life at home was quite regimented and horses were the children's escape.

Figure 25: Claude Odlum, M.F.H. of Kildare Hounds with daughters Corinne (l) and Mavis (r): 1930

Mavis, the youngest, who was beautiful and clever, was sent to stay with a family in Canada when she was about 18. Unfortunately, she became ill and was sent home to recuperate. Despite having her 21st. birthday party at the Savoy Hotel in London, her health continued to deteriorate and she was forced to give up a secretarial course in London and return to *Leinster Grove*. Tragically, she was diagnosed with TB and died a few months later.

Corinne lived at *Leinster Grove* after leaving school - she too suffered from poor health and was not very strong. During WWII, she worked for the Women's Voluntary Service in London and it was on leave back in Co. Kildare in the winter of 1944 that she met her future husband, John Millard, who was a Lt. Colonel on the staff of XXX Corps and had earlier taken part in the D-Day landing in France. They married in September 1945 and spent the rest of their lives in Africa, first in Tanzania (then Tanganyika) and later in Kenya.

Figure 26: Mavis, Corinne and Audrey

Doris was a very keen fisherwoman and Claude purchased an estate at Inver in Connemara in 1941. It contained a number of sea trout lakes, a fish hatchery as well as a number of houses. Its remoteness was both an attraction and a disadvantage in

Figure 27: Claude & Doris Odlum pictured on steps of Leinster Grove. Source: Henry Simon Ltd. Occasional Letter, October 1957

that it was time consuming to access and manage. The property was later sold off but the Millards did retain a section of the eastern part of the estate.

Algernon's business acumen was obviously recognized as he was appointed to the Board of a number of State-owned companies. As well as being a Director of the Irish Wallboard Company in Athy, he was also a Director of the Irish Sugar Company (who would eventually purchase the Odlum flour milling business in the late 1980s) from November 1937 to 1949, becoming Chairman in that year. He and Chippie lived in some splendour in Kilnacourt - a relic of Edwardian times, with a small coterie of household staff and a strict hierarchical order. It was very much an 'Upstairs Downstairs' environment – even the visitng churchwarden from the local church and the vet had to present themselves at the tradesmen's entrance for admission. There were two men working outside, one who doubled up as a driver (Algernon never drove) and the other with responsibility for the garden and ensuring that the gravel in the driveway was perfectly raked. Two Jersey cows were kept in the fields behind the house - these pampered animals provided milk and cream for the household.

Unable to buy spares for their Mercedes car during the war, Algernon purchased a Bentley.

There is an amusing anecdote that the driver, Fedigan, at one stage drew their attention to holes in the carpet in the rear of this vehicle. It transpired that with the car parked in a garage at some distance from the house, the locals were gaining access to it and using it as a trysting spot. The holes in the carpet were the result of cigarettes being stubbed out in it by the visiting couples!

Figure 28: Audrey and Corinne Odlum, Leinster Grove: 1943

Figure 29: Doris Odlum with 3 1/2 lb trout caught at Inver ca. 1965

In later years, after Algernon's death, Chippie took to driving herself. She was used to being 'Queen of the Road' and expected others to get out of her way. There were stories of locals diving for cover on the narrow Pass bridge over the River Barrow just outside Monasterevin as she sailed majestically by in the car.[26] Family etiquette also ruled that if other family members had the misfortune of getting behind her on the drive up to Dublin, they were expected to stay behind. Overtaking was frowned upon!

The house was managed by three staff - a cook and two maids. The kitchen had only the most basic of equipment - none of the labour saving devices that are now commonplace were available; everything was done by hand. That did not prevent the menu being adventurous for its day - asparagus, artichokes, bottled water were served long before they became everyday items in Ireland. 'Proper' table manners were expected, with the full array of cutlery placed on the table including fruit knives and forks which were required for peeling the skins off the fruit - a skill in itself.

Chapter 7:
The Fourth Generation

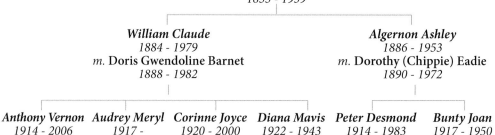

WILLIAM PERRY
1844 - 1922

m. **Emma Harriet Podger**
1855 - 1939

William Claude *1884 - 1979* *m.* Doris Gwendoline Barnet *1888 - 1982*	*Algernon Ashley* *1886 - 1953* *m.* Dorothy (Chippie) Eadie *1890 - 1972*

Anthony Vernon *1914 - 2006*	*Audrey Meryl* *1917 -*	*Corinne Joyce* *1920 - 2000*	*Diana Mavis* *1922 - 1943*	*Peter Desmond* *1914 - 1983*	*Bunty Joan* *1917 - 1950*

RICHARD EDWARD
1849 - 1924

m. **Jane Eleanor Hinds**
1855 - 1919

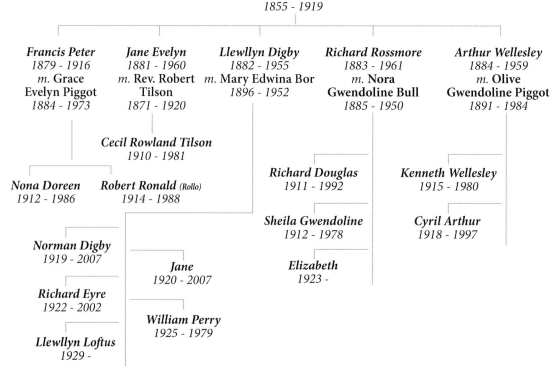

Francis Peter *1879 - 1916* *m.* Grace Evelyn Piggot *1884 - 1973*	*Jane Evelyn* *1881 - 1960* *m.* Rev. Robert Tilson *1871 - 1920*	*Llewllyn Digby* *1882 - 1955* *m.* Mary Edwina Bor *1896 - 1952*	*Richard Rossmore* *1883 - 1961* *m.* **Nora** Gwendoline Bull *1885 - 1950*	*Arthur Wellesley* *1884 - 1959* *m.* **Olive** Gwendoline Piggot *1891 - 1984*

Cecil Rowland Tilson
1910 - 1981

Richard Douglas
1911 - 1992

Kenneth Wellesley
1915 - 1980

Nona Doreen
1912 - 1986

Robert Ronald (Rollo)
1914 - 1988

Sheila Gwendoline
1912 - 1978

Cyril Arthur
1918 - 1997

Norman Digby
1919 - 2007

Jane
1920 - 2007

Elizabeth
1923 -

Richard Eyre
1922 - 2002

William Perry
1925 - 1979

Llewllyn Loftus
1929 -

The Fourth Generation

A new business format was established on 29 March 1935 when W.P. & R. Odlum Limited was formed with a capital of 270,000 shares at £1 each fully paid. This joint stock format replaced the now outmoded partnership model. This company acquired the businesses carried on by W.P. & R. Odlum in Portarlington, Portlaoise and St. Mullin's and Odlum & Odlum in Naas and Sallins. The Directors were Claude and Algernon, who each held 67,500 shares and Willie, Digby, Arthur and Ross who each held 33,750. Claude was appointed as Chairman, Willie as Deputy Chairman and Algernon as Managing Director.[1]

On the business side, guaranteed prices for flour that had been established under the Cereals Act proved a boon for the milling industry but the government sponsored drive to increase the acreage under wheat brought its own problems. It soon became clear that the milling industry was being protected for the benefit of the agricultural community rather than the millers. Much of the additional wheat was grown in areas unsuitable for the cultivation of milling wheat which required warm, dry conditions. In a bid to find a market for this grain, the government steadily increased the amounts of home grown wheat that had to be used by the Irish mills from 35% in 1938-9 to almost 95% in 1941.[2] This led to increased costs for the millers who had to pay for a product that they could not use as well as importing expensive wheat from Canada and Australia to supplement the poor quality native crop. Flour prices rose as a result, giving vent to discontent amongst consumers and politicians with calls from the Labour party in 1938 to bring the milling industry under state control.

Indeed this was to be a feature of the political and industrial climate for most of the next two decades. Farmers accused the Irish millers of having no interest in purchasing their wheat, politicians accused the millers of serving their own interests and lining their own pockets and all this took place against a background of declining flour consumption.

Figure 30: Advertisement encouraging wheat growing. Source: Free State Farmer, Nov. 1936

The Fourth Generation

At the same time, members of the next generation were finding employment within the business. A total of nine individuals from this generation would work at various levels within the company. To distinguish one from the other at work, each was addressed by their first name, with the more formal 'Mr.' added.

Douglas, son of Ross, took over the mill in St. Mullin's during the early 1930s. Cecil Tilson, son of Evie, worked in Portlaoise and Ken, elder son of Arthur, started in Naas, working under the direction of Claude. Cecil undertook his initial milling training in Thompsons flour mill in Hull, England. This was followed by a spell with MIAG, milling engineers of Braunschweig, Germany who, at that time, were installing grain handling equipment in a number of the Odlum mills. He started working with Odlums in 1933, focusing on the technical side of the business.

Perhaps the most significant new player was Peter Odlum, son of Algernon and Chippie, who started in the Dublin Port Mill in 1936 at the age of 22. Educated at Baymount in Clontarf, he followed in his father's footsteps, completing his secondary education at Charterhouse School, in Godalming, west of London. This was followed by a stint in Oxford. However, he did not graduate, finding the rigours of studying difficult to deal with. He was the first family member to work in the Dublin Port Mill, ensuring that the family interests were represented and applying a level of financial control that had been previously lacking. He was soon immersed in the politics and strategy of the milling industry in Ireland attending his first IFMA meeting in July 1944. As the heir apparent, the balance of power was to stay within the orbit

Figure 31: Three generations together Richard (sitting), Arthur (standing), Cyril (front), Ken (behind) ca. 1923

Figure 32 (Left): Peter Odlum pictured with his grandmother, Emma Odlum, at Marjorie Graham's wedding, London, 1937

of the families of Algernon and Claude Odlum. As in previous generations, these families had little interaction with the 'other' side - the descendants of Richard and Jane Odlum.

The year 1939 marked the arrival of two more of Richard's family members into the business. Cyril, younger son of Arthur and Olive and Norman, eldest son of Digby and Mary, both joined in September of that year. Norman had attended Trinity College, Dublin but had failed the Final Freshman Examination (popularly known as 'Little-Go' and a stumbling block for many students) at the end of his second year. He then took up employment in Odlums, initially being assigned to the grain intake in Gilbeys, Portlaoise who handled the wheat storage for the mill in Portlaoise. By this time, war had broken out in Europe. Faced with the boredom of looking at wheat all day against what was popularly portrayed (at least in the British media) as the excitement and adventure of the campaign, Norman decided to join the British forces. Whether this was a spontaneous decision is not clear but he failed to inform Lew Sharpe, the General Manager, of his resolve. Having seen Norman on the previous Friday, when asked on the following Monday where Norman was, he was told: 'Oh, didn't you hear, he's joined up!' [3]

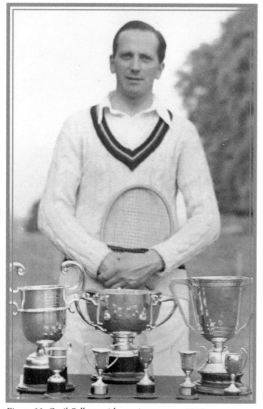

Figure 33: Cyril Odlum with tennis cups - ca. 1947

Figure 34: Cyril Odlum in Connaught hockey strip ca. 1942

After travelling north to Belfast to enlist, Norman was initially stationed in the camp in Ballykinlar, Co. Down for training. He was transferred to Catterick in North Yorkshire and finally to Devizes, Wiltshire for officer training from where he was commissioned as a 2nd. Lieutenant in the Duke of Wellington's 4th. Battalion - an anti-tank unit.

After leaving school in Campbell College, Belfast, Cyril completed his milling training with Hosegoods in Bath. His father, Arthur, had bought him an open top MG sports car, so he must have cut a dash even at this early stage in his life. Returning to Portlaoise in 1939, he started work in the mill. With Lew Sharpe in charge of the overall operation, this provided Cyril with the opportunity to indulge in his sporting activities where he enjoyed considerable success, winning many tennis tournaments and representing Connaught in hockey.

The next member of the family to join the business was Richard (Dick) Odlum, second son of Digby and Mary who joined in 1940, having completed his education in St. Columba's College, Dublin. Working in the mill office would not have come naturally to Dick's independent spirit - he was more focused on motoring * and social events. One particular incident reveals Dick's own particular initiative. An event in Parknasilla, Co. Kerry saw Dick vying with a number of other potential suitors for the attention of a particular female. At the end of the event all the male rivals were departing, leaving the object of their desire behind at the hotel.

Determined to outfox his rivals, he got on the train in Kenmare in view of the others but as they awaited the train's departure, Dick surreptitiously slipped out of the carriage on the opposite side. He hightailed it back to Parknasilla but, unfortunately, his romantic approaches were rebuffed and the potential conquest never happened.[4]

Perhaps in a bid to temper his disappointment, Dick then purchased a 250 c.c. Triumph motorbike. Although bought secondhand, it was sent to Erne Motors in Baggot Street, Dublin for a complete overhaul and rechrome - all done at his father's expense. But even this was not enough excitement as both he and Cyril became somewhat disillusioned with life in Portlaoise. Perhaps knowing that he was only playing second fiddle may have compounded things for Dick. This was illustrated by an incident in Portlaoise where Dick met Algernon in the street. Dick went to shake Algernon's hand as they passed by. Although they were work colleagues, albeit at a different level, Algernon walked straight past him, ignoring his outstretched hand! [5]

War service

Like Norman, both Cyril and Dick were drawn to the events in Europe and in 1943, they too decided to join up with the British forces. Travelling across the border into Northern Ireland, they enlisted in the R.A.F. They both undertook their elementary flying training which included a basic ground course in Morse code. This was problematic for Dick and proved to be the end of his attempts to become a pilot. Cyril progressed to an Elementary Flying Training School for preliminary flight training. However, the wider Empire Flight Training Scheme (EFTS) had been so successful that at this stage in the war, there was actually a surfeit of pilots and only two of his class went on to advanced pilot training. Instead, Cyril went to gunnery school in Pembroke,

* Loftus Odlum (youngest son of Digby and Mary) recalls a noteable event just before the introduction of petrol rationing during the Emergency (as the WWII period was known in Ireland) when Dick drove him (aged about 14) and Cyril from Portlaoise to Limerick, Killarney, Cork (where they went to the theatre) and back to Portlaoise - all in the one day, returning home at 3 a.m. !

Figure 35: Cyril Odlum in uniform, ca. 1944

Figure 36: Dick Odlum in the cockpit of a Spitfire, Mingaladon, Burma ca. 1947

Figure 37: Norman Odlum in dress uniform ca. 1945

Figure 38: Peter Odlum in uniform ca. 1945

Wales but the end of the war in Europe came before he had completed his training. Offered the chance to demob in 1945, he took it and returned to Ireland and his former job.

Dick switched from flying to transport, completing a course in Blackpool on driving trucks. At the end of the war in Europe, Dick was based in Kirton in Lindsey in Lincolnshire, again, like Cyril, not having seen active service. The life seemed to suit Dick as when he too was offered the chance to demob, he turned it down, preferring to stay in the services. He was posted to R.A.F. Mingaladon, Burma (now Myanmar) where he spent most of his time driving a petrol bowser refueling aircraft. With the coming of independence in Burma and the scaling back of RAF activities, Dick was demobbed and returned to Ireland in 1947 *'brown as a berry'.**

Unlike his brother and cousin, Norman was in the thick of the conflict. Transferred to Egypt in 1943 as part of the 8th. Army, he took part in the North African campaign against Rommel's Afrika Korps and was later involved in the Allied forces landing in Salerno, Italy. This was followed by the long slog up through Italy where he was to remain for the rest of the war. With the end of combat in the European theatre, he was transferred first to Haifa in Palestine and later finished out his service in Graz, Austria from where in 1946, as an acting Major, he was demobbed.[6]

Peter chose to stay in Ireland during the war years and joined the Maritime Inscription or Irish Naval Reserve. Their task was to assist in protecting the Irish ports and fisheries - a number of motor torpedo boats (MTB's) were purchased for this purpose. Peter was the only family member to serve with the Irish forces - perhaps this was an attempt to establish an Irish identity for a family who were generally perceived as English or *'West Brit'* in their outlook. With the war now over, and all the serving members back at home, things returned more or less to normal in the business. Cyril slotted back into his role in the mill in Portlaoise, Dick resumed his duties in the office and Norman was sent to Waterford to assist Alan Harris in running the operation there. Both Cyril and Dick made sure that they had sufficient time off to pursue their hobbies with Cyril going on the competitive tennis circuit during the summer months. Among his victories was the doubles competition in June 1948 at the British and Irish Millers convention in Scarborough, Yorkshire partnered by a Mrs. Alexander.[7]

The year 1948 also saw the building of new steel silos in the Dublin Port Mill, supplied by MIAG of Germany, to store the increasing quantities of native wheat that was being grown. This again was a major construction project due to the ground conditions and required an extensive piling programme to ensure a proper foundation for the structure. An additional storage capacity of 16,000 tonnes was added at a cost of £280,000. Further storage capacity was added in 1955 with the construction of a grain drying and storage facility in Ardee, Co. Meath, funded by a loan from the Department of Agriculture.[8]

Although flour consumption rose immediately at the end of the war due to shortages of other foods, the 1950s marked a low point in the Irish economy. Lack of job opportunities in a stagnant manufacturing sector and declining agricultural output resulted in significant emigration from the country. The old protectionist policies had reached their limits. What

* As remembered by his brother, Loftus Odlum.

Figure 39: Piling for new wheat silos, Dublin Port Mill, 1948

industry that did exist was of small scale, often far removed from its supply of raw materials and the end user of its finished products. One criticism of the Fianna Fáil protectionist policies is that they had led to the encouragement of an excessive number of small, weak firms that were ill equipped to face increasing competition.

The 1950s was also to witness the passing of much of the third generation of the milling Odlums. Willie died in March 1950 aged 72, having spent the last two years of his life in Glenageary, Co. Dublin. In the same year Algernon suffered a stroke which affected his speech and he too died in May 1953, aged 67. Digby died in 1955, aged 73, Arthur in 1959, aged 75 and finally, Ross in December 1961, aged 78. Claude remained as Chairman but Peter, who had been admitted to the partnership in October 1949, took over the reins from his father and assumed the role of Managing Director, guiding and directing the business from his base in the Dublin Port Mill. Somewhat aloof, Peter was a commanding figure, significantly taller than most of his Odlum cousins and marked out by his trademark handkerchief in the breast pocket of his jacket and his cheroots.

Other management changes included the appointment of John (Jock) Scott in 1951 to the position of General Manager in Portlaoise in place of Lew Sharpe, who had died that year. Scott had previously been General Manager of the Grand Canal Co., from 1937 to 1950 at which stage it was taken over by CIE and effectively nationalized.[9]

Two additional Odlum family members also took up employment with the company during the period. Having completed three years training with Hulberts in Hulme, Manchester, Loftus took up the position as Assistant Mill Manager in the Dublin Port Mill in October 1950, in place of Bob Ladley, who moved across the river Liffey, as Mill Manager of the Dock Mill. In 1954, Loftus moved to Portarlington as Mill Manager, a position he was to hold for 39 years, retiring in 1999. Rollo, who had graduated from Trinity College, Dublin and qualified as an accountant with Craig Gardner, took on the role of Company Secretary in 1952.

One other family achievement from the 1950s that deserves mention was Dick's short but stellar motor racing career. With assistance from his father, Digby, in 1952 Dick purchased

Figure 40: Dick and Loftus Odlum pictured in St. Helier, Jersey 1947

Figure 41: Dick Odlum's Frazer Nash car racing at Goodwood (?): 1952

a single-seater Frazer Nash racing car. After a couple of sorties with the car in England, Dick concentrated on events in Ireland competing in all the events in the racing calendar, including hill climbs. Modifications made to the car at the end of season improved its performance. This extra speed meant that 1953 was a good year, as Dick won the Sexton Trophy which was presented by the Royal Irish Automobile Club for the best performance by an Irish driver.

The highlight of 1954, which was arguably Dick's best season, was his victory at the Curragh in September, in the last race of the season. * Dick won the race by 20 seconds at an average speed of 67.41 m.ph. [10] But motor racing was becoming more professional and the days of the amateur 'privateer' were numbered. Nor did Dick have the time or inclination to commit to days of car testing, which was becoming increasingly important in terms of achieving results.

So 1955 was to prove to be the final year of his racing driving adventures. It was to be a momentous end - driving in one of the most famous motor races in the world, the Le Mans 24 Hours. Dick drove a works Frazer Nash Sebring as co-driver to Cecil Vard. Unfortunately, Dick managed to complete only one lap as the car was forced to retire with mechanical damage on lap 33. Ironically it was on the subsequent lap that, following a collision with a slowing car in front, the Mercedes Benz driven by French driver, Pierre Levegh, was catapulted into the crowd, creating the worst motor racing accident of all time with more than 80 fatalities. [11]

Dick's own Frazer Nash was sent back to their works, which were by coincidence also

* This proved to be the last event ever held on the circuit, as a fatality on the track led to the closure of the venue on safety grounds

in Isleworth and that was the end of his racing exploits. There were different priorities in Dick's life at this stage as he had recently got married (May 1954) and his new bride, Patricia Hogan, was not keen to see her new partner put his life and their future together, at risk.

If Dick's passion was motoring and Cyril's tennis, then Peter's was boats, especially yachts. Peter owned a number of racing yachts during his lifetime and was a member of the Royal Irish Yacht Club for many years. He was elected Rear-Commodore in 1959 and later served as Commodore for a four year stint from 1972 to 1976.[12] His first yacht was named 'Maureen' - a 21 foot racer. This was followed by a series of 8 metre yachts first based in Dun Laoghaire and later on the Clyde in Scotland. In July 1964, he registered the remarkable achievement of 10 wins out of 12 starts in his yacht 'Inismara' during Clyde Fortnight. [13]

Figure 42: Peter Odlum at helm of 'Maureen',
Irish Times, 22 August 1939

This period also witnessed a series of weddings with Dick's brothers, Norman and Loftus marrying in 1946 and 1952 respectively, Cyril ('the catch of the county' [14]) in 1957 and Rollo in 1958. Indicative of the relaxed times in which they were working, Dick spent nearly eight weeks on his honeymoon in the south of France, driving there in a reconditioned Austin A-40 which had had the bumpers replaced as the original ones were not up to scratch!

At the same time, Ranks was also extending its reach through the acquisition of a number of bakeries in Dublin, Cork and Kilcock, Co. Meath. This tied-bakery arrangement had become a popular format in the UK and introduced a level of vertical integration that provided a guaranteed market for the flour produced by the milling arm. Johnston Mooney & O'Brien had been an early exponent of this business model with a flour mill in Jones Road on the northside of Dublin and bakeries on the other side of the river in Ballsbridge and Leinster Street.

To counteract this expansion by Ranks, Odlums assessed potential acquisitions in the bakery sector. This brought Johnston Mooney and O'Brien into the spotlight -whose bread bakery in Ballsbridge stood on a 5 ½ acre freehold site along with a number of retail outlets around Dublin. Due to their Directors' conservative dividend policy, the company's share price was quite low, making it an attractive takeover target. An offer was made for the shares on 26 November 1956. The bid was successful with nearly 95% shareholders accepting the offer, with the purchase price set at around £450,000 in total. This proved to be something of a coup as the stocks of grain in the flour mill was valued at £441,000, meaning that the deal was almost self financing. [15]

Having considered a move to Canada where a job in the Rootes motor company had been secured for him, Dick now decided that his future lay in Ireland. With increasing competition emerging in a long-dormant flour milling industry, Odlums moved to counter increasingly aggressive moves by Ranks in the retail and wholesale markets. As Ranks had entered into the Midlands area - a traditional stronghold for Odlums - in a tit-for-tat move Odlums decided to move into Ranks home town of Limerick and the surrounding areas. Dick was picked by John Scott to spearhead this drive and Dick's sociable nature and outgoing personality proved to be a major contributing factor to the success of the venture.

So Odlums moved in the 1960s well placed to see off the challenges that were to face it over the next decade.

Figure 43: Rollo and Cyril pictured outside Rockview ca. 1955 with the Austin A40 Devon they raced in 1949 Circuit of Ireland Trial

Chapter 8:
Consolidation and Rationalization

The initial increase in flour consumption that immediately followed the end of the Emergency/WWII period, soon gave way to an inexorable decline in flour sales. Increased emigration, changing family structures and growing urbanization were all contributing factors. Annual per capita consumption of flour fell from 300lbs in 1945 to 220lbs in 1958 with a corresponding decline in production from 411,000 metric tonnes in 1945 to 270,000 in 1965.[1]

A government report, commissioned in 1962 but only published in 1966, reported that there was an excess of 50% in the production capacity of the flour milling industry. It recommended the abolition of the quota system which would allow the natural forces of competition to determine which mills remained in production and what the output of each would be.[2]

But the inevitable process of rationalization within the industry was already well under way - something that de Valera's protectionist policies had merely postponed by a period of 20 years. The flour millers took the initiative themselves by setting up a voluntary rationalization programme which was funded by a levy on members of the IFMA. First to close were the smallest and least efficient mills - some of which were to close for a second time, having shut in the 1920s and been reopened under the licensing system introduced by the Fianna Fáil government in the 1930s. This policy had focused more on employment opportunities rather than strict economic criteria. Symptomatic of this was the construction of a new mill in Ballina which had opened in July 1936, only to close its doors in April 1964, a mere 28 years later. The fact that the subsidy on bread and flour introduced during the Emergency was withdrawn in May 1957 and that large quantities of poor quality Irish grown wheat still had to be incorporated into the milling grist, did not help the millers' cause.[3]

Mill closures

As part of the industry sponsored rationalization programme six mills agreed to exit the industry in 1960. A further ten mills closed between 1962 and 1965, including the Odlums mill in St. Mullin's in 1962 [4], as part of an extended scheme at a total cost of £522,611 and additional pension payments of £125,209.[5] Amongst the mills that closed during this period was the Johnston Money & O'Brien plant in Jones Road (now owned by Odlums) which suffered an explosion and subsequent devastating fire on the night of 3 October 1961 (fig. 36). Thankfully there were no fatalities but the mill was almost completely destroyed. Given the cost of reconstruction and the level of excess capacity within the industry, it was decided not to rebuild it. The milling licence was transferred to the Dublin Port Mill and a guaranteed annual sale of 83,000 sacks (10,540 metric tonnes) of flour to the bakery agreed.[6]

This left a total of 17 operating mills at this stage, with Odlums operating seven of these and Ranks four. Of the six remaining independent mills, three were in Dublin - Bolands, Dock and Shackelton (in Lucan) with Milford in Donegal, Barrow Mills in Carlow and S. & A.G. Davis in Enniscorthy making up the balance. With all these closures, the sales quotas under the licencing system were amended with the independents' share reduced to 27.45%, from 34%, Ranks increasing from 30% to 32.67% and Odlums increasing from 36% to 39.88% - making them the dominant player in the market.[7]

Figure 44: Fire at Johnston Mooney & O'Brien mill, 1961, Milling, 13 Oct 1961, p. 351

All of this took place against a background of calls by TDs Noel Browne and Jack McQuillan to nationalize the flour milling industry. This was inspired by a move to reduce the price of bread and in the face of what they saw as unnecessary job losses and near monopoly profits for those millers that remained in the industry. The matter was debated in the Dail on 24 November 1960, but the motion was defeated by 41 votes to 60 with votes going along party lines, with the government (Fianna Fáil) voting against and the opposition for the proposal.

Associated Mills

In the face of these changes within the industry, the Odlums had consolidated their position by restructuring their business and extending their shareholding into other flour mills. This aligned them further with families that already had common shareholdings in the Dublin Port Mill, such as the Halls, Kennedys and Figgis. A new company, Associated Mills Ltd. was formed in 1962 with Odlums as the major shareholder at 58%, Halls with 18%, Kennedys 6% and Figgis 5% and a number of smaller shareholders holding the balance.[8] Claude and Peter Odlum represented the family's interest as Directors of the new company. This now gave Odlums access to the Cork market through a shareholding in the National Flour Mills in Cork and in the west of Ireland through a shareholding in Pollexfens in Ballisodare, Co. Sligo. With the closure of St. Mullin's in 1962, Odlums were now operating flour mills in Dublin, Cork, Portlaoise, Portarlington, Naas, Waterford and Ballisodare and an oatmeal mill in Sallins.

Despite the closures elsewhere, there was increased investment in the Dublin Port Mill with the installation of new grain, flour packing and storage facilities in a purpose built silo. This was provided by MIAG of Germany and was completed in 1960.[9] In addition, a diversification into animal feeds took place with the formation of a new company, Bestock Farm Foods Ltd. which was incorporated in 1962 and a provender mill installed in the premises to supply this business.[10]

Even so, for the members of the Odlum family life continued at a leisurely pace. For many, work was a sociable event which started at 10 o'clock in the morning, followed by a break for lunch when everyone went home for a sit down meal and then a return to the office for a period in the afternoon. Ken, Arthur's elder son, who was based in the Naas mill, stayed in Lawlor's Hotel in the town during the week, returning to the family home in *Rockview* in Portlaoise for the weekends. For the country folk a day off mid-week for a visit to 'town' (Dublin) was not uncommon and during the summer months Thursday afternoons were spent in a privately owned tennis club in Portlaoise. The tennis was a relaxed affair but competition was intense amongst female family members to produce the best teas that featured an impressive arrays of homemade sandwiches and cakes.

Peter Odlum, who served two terms as president of the IFMA during the 1960s, also devoted considerable time to his sailing. Racing on the Clyde occupied most weekends during the competitive season, with the crew flying over to Glasgow on a Friday and returning on a Sunday evening. Peter would also spend his summer holidays in Scotland boating - a break of two to three weeks duration.

Although a sizeable rationalisation programme has already been undertaken during the 1960s, there was still significant excess capacity within the flour milling industry. Declining sales of flour in Ireland, combined with the ever present threat of cheap imports, ramped up the pressure on the industry. With accession to the E.E.C. (now EU) in 1973, following an original adjustment period what was a protected industry became exposed for the first time to the rigours of full competition. An attempt to merge the interests of Odlums and Ranks in 1974 was scuppered by government concerns over a potential monopoly situation in the flour milling sector and was shelved. On the one hand, the government was keen to resolve the ongoing overcapacity within the industry but on the other, ran scared of the decreased level of competition that this would entail. Ranks then announced their intention to phase out

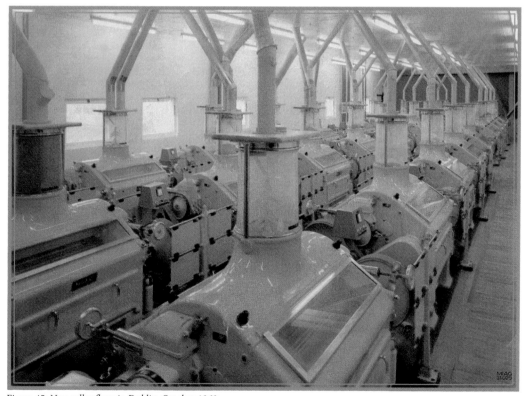

Figure 45: New roller flour in Dublin, October 1969

flour and animal feed production in Limerick over an 18 month period. Following repeated representations from the government and other interested parties, the company agreed to continue operating the flour mill.

Odlums mill closures

Clearly it was uneconomic to operate six Odlum mills - many of them small scale, so a programme of mill closures was put in place during the 1970s. Ballisodare closed in 1974, Portlaoise and Waterford were closed in 1977 and finally Naas in 1978.[11] During this period the operating company name changed from Associated Mills, to Odlum Mills Limited in 1974 and Odlum Group Limited in 1977.

Figure 46: Exterior of 1903 mill in Portarlington, prior to demolition (note the canal section that ran alongside the mill is now filled in)

In a move that probably guaranteed its survival, Odlums embarked on a programme of modernization in its remaining mills, aided in part by government grants. Dublin had already been significantly upgraded in 1969 with the installation of a new MIAG plant, which replaced the existing Simon mill that dated from 1948. This new mill had a capacity of 70 sacks per hour (or 300 tons of wheat per 24 hours, as they are now currently rated) and significantly more automated than the one that it replaced. The 78 roller mills in the old mill were reduced to 27 in the new mill, with a corresponding reduction in the floor space used. An article by M. Grimminger, MIAG's Chief Engineer of the day, described the building in these terms. 'A carefully matched color scheme of plant and building, generous fluorescent lighting and sealed parquet floors provide a pleasant atmosphere.'[12] Operating costs were reduced by a lowering of the manning levels from five men per shift to two.

In Portarlington, in the years prior to 1973, investment in the mill had been mostly in warehousing, bulk storage, packing and transport. There had been little expenditure on the mill itself and it was becoming expensive to maintain and operate.

A modern milling plant could be operated in a smaller building with a much smaller work force and at the same time produce a much bigger output. To put the site on a competitive footing, it was decided to demolish the existing mill and replace it with a custom-built building to house a new plant - a Simon 40 sack/170 tonnes of wheat per 24 hours. This was going to be the first new mill built in Ireland since 1935. The old mill was closed down on 17 June 1977 and the new one commenced production on 7 September 1978, all in the space of 15 months. During the period of construction, flour was transferred from the mill in Portlaoise to Portarlington for packing off.

Harry Bantry White, the mill manager, did trojan work in keeping the process of installing the new plant moving forward. A productivity deal was negotiated with the unions that included a severance settlement for a number of workers who left under the scheme and fixed a new rate for those remaining. The workforce was reduced from about 80 in earlier years to 40.[13]

Cork was the last mill to be updated with the work undertaken in the period 1981/2 and a new Simon 60 sack/250 tonnes of wheat per 24 hours installed in a new purpose-built structure built by Collen Bros. of Dublin. Construction was delayed as the building workers went on strike during the build, delaying the completion of the project by a number of weeks. Additional bulk flour storage space was also added, coming on stream in 1983.

The 1970s brought with it a series of challenges. A National Prices Commission was established in 1971 which regulated the price for both flour and bread. This introduced a level of rigidity into the market where there was often a considerable time lag between the submissions by the flour millers and the eventual granting of price increases by the Commission. Not all applications were successful and in some instances prices were actually reduced.

A further threat came in 1976 from attempts made by one of the supermarket chains to import 'own label' flour from outside the jurisdiction. Up to this point the Irish millers had only supplied their own brands to the retail trade. Reluctantly, a decision was taken to pack for the retail chains- at a much reduced profit margin. Within a short period of time, this trade accounted for 11.7% of the small pack volume.[14]

By the end of the decade, there were only 12 members left in the IFMA and 4 of these were 'honorary' members from Northern Ireland. In 1974, S. & A.G. Davis took over the production quota of W.H. Mosse following the merger of the two business and the subsequent closure of the latter's mill. In March 1978, Ranks closed their Cork mill. Outside the Odlums restructuring of their business, the only other modernization programme was undertaken by Bolands who planned to expand their capacity with the installation of a new 60 sack mill in 1978 in their premises in Ringsend, Dublin.

The mid 1970s probably marked the highwater mark for Odlums in terms of profitability. An article in the *Irish Press* in April 1977 referred to profits of £2.5 million for the 12-month period of 1976 (equivalent to ca. £15 million in today's values). This placed the company 'well up the list of the Top Ten Irish companies for profits.'[15] Increased competition and higher costs meant that the company struggled to sustain this level of return over subsequent years.

Chapter 9:
Marketing and Material Culture

Having examined the physical aspects of the business - mills and milling - and the individuals who worked in it, it is worth looking at other aspects of the operation, namely the marketing and distribution of the finished product.

Irish industry, in general, was slow to adopt the principles of branding and marketing. Concepts that were widely used in the U.S. in the 1920s were only accepted and implemented in Ireland in the 1960s. Many businesses in Ireland saw advertising as merely a vulgar intrusion. This may in part be explained by the legacy of the Quaker families who dominated Irish industry during the latter part of the nineteenth century and the early part of the twentieth century - for example, Shackeltons and Goodbodys in flour, Bewleys in tea and coffee and Jacobs in biscuit baking. The Quaker ethos and principles would not have countenanced such brazen public display.

Instead, the focus was on producing the best product - technical and engineering capabilities were prized over selling skills. In a sense, a belief prevailed that if the product was good enough, it would sell itself. For Odlums it was no different- most of those who joined the business had done some form of milling training, normally through placement with one of the English millers.

Nevertheless, there were still initiatives to support local industry. As already mentioned (see Chapter 5), one of the few early initiatives to promote flour centred around the use of the Déanta in Éirinn symbol. This promoted the purchase of Irish made products and was particularly appropriate given the high level of cheaper imports that were coming in to the country. This was primarily targeted at shopkeepers to encourage them to stock Irish-made products in their stores and to promote the use of Irish milled flour in the bakery trade.

Much of the advertising in the early years of the century was of a business-to-business type, rather than business to consumer. This is illustrated by a series of advertisements placed by Irish flour millers in a feature on the Irish flour milling industry published in the 25 October 1924 edition of *Milling* magazine.

Figure 47: Déanta in Éirinn symbol

Figure 48: Odlums advertisements placed in October 1924 edition of Milling magazine

Figure 49: Advertisement for Odlums Irish Purity Flour. Milling, 24 October 1924.

In keeping with the tone of the period, the emphasis is on the production facilities and the products produced. There is no reference to the consumer.

However, it was in the designs of the cotton flour sacks used to pack flour for the wholesale and retail trades that the flour milling trade showed originality and innovation. These polychrome bags appeared to be unique to the flour trade as most other products were packed in bags featuring just a single colour. For their inspiration in design, many looked back to the time of the Celtic Revival, a Victorian movement that spanned the years 1850 -1920 and explored the culture of Ireland pre-conquest and reappraised its craft and designs. In a sense, this was an additional way in promoting the 'Irishness' of the product albeit with a backward glance into history and a revival of the past.

Two designs for Odlums products (sadly by unknown graphic artists) drew heavily of these symbols of a Gaelic past. The Odlums 'Cream' sack (fig. 50) depicts a round tower - a symbol of antiquity, endurance and durability - surrounded by a garland of wheat grains and shamrock (another Gaelic motif). An interesting, although maybe not immediately apparent, logo device is used with the initials 'W'. 'P' & 'R' 'O' intertwined denoting W.P. and R. Odlum. Some of the text is designed in such a way as to mimic a Gaelic font, particularly in the word 'Cream'.

The second design features the image of Erin which had been used to embody the country of Ireland in nineteenth century political cartoons, particularly in publications such as the *Illustrated London News*. In many of these images Erin is portrayed as the essence of domesticity, dressed in white and green and complemented by a red cloak. This is obviously the inspiration for the image used in the design for '*Irish Purity*'(fig 49) flour which was produced in the Portarlington mill. It could be argued that, in this instance, Erin is adopting a somewhat coquettish pose!

But there is another aspect to these cotton sacks which makes them unique. Although probably motivated more by economic necessity than any environmental considerations, the potential of the high quality cotton material used in the construction of the sacks became apparent. These cotton bags were sold into both the wholesale and retail trade. The 10 stone (63 kilos approx.) and 8 stone (50kg approx.) bags were a popular size with rural households. The flour, in turn, would be decanted into a bin and stored for use, leaving the sack available for alternative purpose. As thrifty households looked for ways to make the best use of limited resources, it was found that four of the larger sacks sewn together made a passable substitute for a bed sheet. As Norman Campion commented:

'Cotton bags were very much a reusable packaging material and few were dumped immediately after being emptied. Many 10/8 stone flour cotton bags became sheets and many a maiden slept between sheets with Purity stamped all over or later when married, the sheets on her side of the bed read Heart's Delight and her husband's Magnificent![*]'

*Purity, Heart's Delight and Magnificent were all brands of flour.

Perhaps the best known anecdote regarding the reuse of flour bags relates to the Kildare GAA football team. Known as the 'Lilywhites', they are reputed to have used recycled 'Lily of the Valley' sacks from Shackleton's mill in Lucan to make up the team kit. (fig. 52).

Initially, the designs were printed directly onto the sacks in a simple process using an ordinary rubber printing block. However, in an interesting example of consumer power, requests were made to the millers to alter the printing process. In her history of Goodbodys of Clara, who were the main producer of cotton sacks in Ireland, Margaret Stewart notes:

'Thrifty Irish housewives used to make shirts, pillow cases and children's clothes from empty cotton flour bags, but they had great difficulty in soaking out the brand and some mothers were said to be embarrassed at seeing their small children advertising someone's brand of flour on the seat of their pants!' [2]

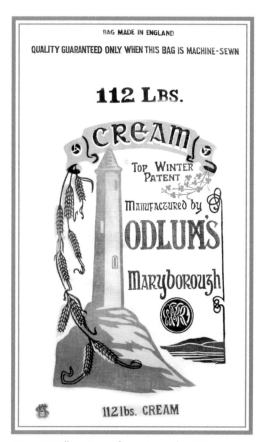

Figure 50: Odlums Cream flour cotton sack c. 1925

Figure 51: Advertisement for Odlum and Odlum. Milling, 24 October 1924.

This problem was overcome through the introduction of 'band labeled' bags where the company and product details were printed on a separate crepe band (fig. 53). This could be easily removed by soaking the cloth in water so that the full piece of material could now be used. Goodbodys also supplied an information leaflet explaining this process.

Figure 52: Postcard illustrating Shackleton's "First Flower of Earth' and 'Lily of the Valley' flours ca. 1940 (N. Campion collection)

Cotton sacks remained in use until the early 1960s when the cost of producing the cotton domestically became uneconomic. Imported cotton had an odour that tainted the flour, resulting in customer complaints - so they were eventually phased out. Rising standards of living also meant that there was less requirement for the recycling of the cloth for making clothing. Paper now took over as the dominant packaging material, as it still remains today.

Figure 53: Band label cotton sack ca. 1960.

The Emergence of Branding and Brand Identity

What little advertising that had been undertaken by the Irish flour millers was mainly of a business-to-business nature with the end consumer often ignored. In fact, promotion was almost seen as an underhand activity as evidenced by minutes of a meeting of the IFMA on 10 February 1938. A complaint had been received of some millers distributing pencils, playing cards, pocket matches etc. among customers for advertising purposes. This should be stopped in the view of some members as this may 'lead to something more expensive.'[3]

The fact that the flour market was strictly controlled from the 1930s onwards and quotas allocated to each of the millers ensured that there was little or no incentive to promote a particular brand, as individual companies were penalized for producing more flour than their allocated quota. What little advertising that was carried out covered a very limited selection of media, newspapers and magazines, outdoor posters (enamel and litho printed), showcards and little else.[4]

But the seeds of change were coming. The key consumer market for flour was under threat as the percentage share of agriculture in the sectoral share of the working population fell from 50% in 1926 to 33% in 1956.[5] Consumption of flour was steadily decreasing - from 300lbs per head in 1945 to 220lbs in 1958.[6] Declining sales exacerbated the situation of excessive capacity within the industry and were to lead to the major shake out amongst the participants that we have already seen.

By 1960, changes were taking place in the marketplace and different consumer demands were emerging. The drivers of these changes were becoming less political and increasingly commercial. The new state was maturing, with the last link with Britain severed through the formation of a Republic of Ireland in 1949. If the 1950s were a period of stagnation, the 1960s marked an important phase in the economic development of Ireland. The time had arrived to

Figure 54: Promotional ink blotter for Odlums Oatmeal ca. 1940

dispense with the now discredited policies of self sufficiency, protectionism and tariffs which had clearly not yielded the benefits that de Valera had promised with their introduction. A different strategy was needed.

The impetus for this change has traditionally been credited to the work of T.K. Whitaker, then Secretary of the Department of Finance, who published in 1957 a survey entitled *Economic Development*. In it he outlined a roadmap for economic progress through significant, targeted capital spending, increased Central Bank power and the encouragement of foreign direct investment aided by incentive packages. Much of what he proposed was incorporated into the first Programme for Economic Expansion which covered the period 1958-1963, which was enthusiastically endorsed by the new leader of Fianna Fáil, Sean Lemass, who succeeded de Valera in 1959.[7]

It was the dawn of a new era where the repression and depression of much of the previous 40 years was swept away. It introduced a new sense of possibility and professionalism into an economy that was growing at an unprecedented rate of 4% p.a.[8]

Restructure in retail

By the 1960s, a retail revolution was also at hand. Food retailing went from traditional counter service operation, epitomized by the Findlater chain of grocery shops, to a self-service, supermarket format. The first Superquinn store opened in Dundalk in 1960 and Dunnes Stores opened in Cornelscourt in 1966. By 1966 half the retail sales in the Leinster area were through self-service outlets.[9]

This meant that consumers now had ultimate discretion over the products they bought. Companies could appeal directly to the end user, so the opportunity to brand products and create a consumer loyalty now presented itself. There was also a requirement for smaller pack sizes as the practice of baking daily was waning. Demand for flour was also weakened by a declining population suffering from enforced emigration.

In the mid-1950s, taking the lead from the UK, Irish millers started to introduce smaller bags of flour in 1lb, 3 ½ lb., 7lb. and 14lb. sizes (fractions of 1 stone), using semi-automated packing machines. There is some debate as who was first to market but it seems to be between 'Dainty' Self Raising flour packed by Walter Brown of Hannover Street, Dublin and 'Tara' brand from Dock Mill.[10] The move away from counter service to self service in the retail trade in the 1960s required flour packed in smaller sizes and delivered direct to the stores. The old-style wholesaler who dealt in the larger 10, 8 and 4 stone cotton sacks went out of business and with their demise, deliveries by rail also ceased.

The first small pack sold by Odlums was 'Fairy' Self Raising flour which was packed

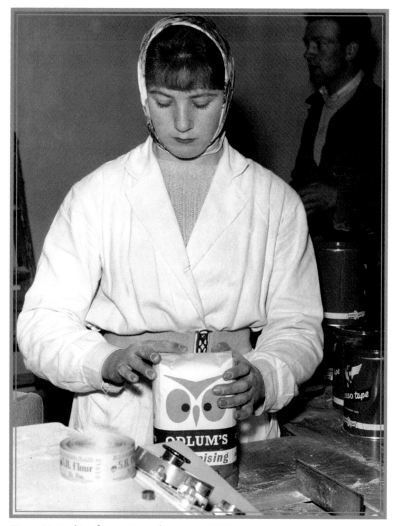

Figure 55: Packing flour in Portarlington ca. 1965

in a 1lb. cellophane bag, featured a design of 2 fairies holding wands which crossed over an image of a baked cake. It was printed in three colours - red, dark blue and yellow [11]. Originally packed in the Sallins mill, a feature on *Co. Kildare's Industrial Story* in the *Irish Independent* of February 10th 1955 extols the product, declaring that it 'makes home baking a pleasure'. The initial packing process was rather primitive with an approximate quantity of flour automatically weighed into the bag, then topped up to the required weight and tied closed with string. Due to significant demand for the product, packing was soon transferred to the Portarlington mill. Fewer men were now required in the mills for handling products formerly packed in cotton sacks but there was a corresponding rise in the number of personnel - initially all female - employed in packing the smaller flour bags.

Professional Graphic Design

During the 1940s and 1950s, due to the political and economic conditions that prevailed in Ireland at the time, few indigenous companies bothered to promote their products. So in 1960, after a break of nearly twenty years, advertising spend in Ireland started to pick up again.

Figure 56: *Wheat Meal flour bags, late 1950s*

Figure 57: *Heart's Delight (made by Odlums) flour bag late 1950s*

Figure 58: *Odlum family crest* *

Ironically, the first major advertising campaign by Guinness in Ireland took place in 1959 and that was only as a result of impending competition from a new brewery being built in Cork.[12] In a move that reflected the change of perspective, in 1959 Jacob's appointed Gordon Lambert to the position of Marketing Director, the first such appointment by an Irish company.

Lambert was one of the early exponents of the primacy of design in all aspects of the company's operation, especially in relation to package design. In the flour milling industry, many of the early designs were borrowed from the company letterheads

* The grant of arms was received in 1929 by W.H. Odlum (1862-1934) of Ardmore, Bray, Co. Wicklow from Sir Neville Wilkinson, the Ulster King of Arms and Principal Herald of all Ireland.

**BETTER BAKING —
BETTER EATING WITH
ODLUM'S CREAM FLOUR**

When you use Odlum's Cream Flour, you can be certain of getting the same high results in your baking all the year round. And because Odlum's Cream Flour never varies in quality—with cakes, pastries, bread — whenever you use flour — it's consistently good.

ODLUM'S
CREAM FLOUR

ODLUM'S
Cream
FLOUR

W. P. & R. ODLUM LTD.

Figure 59: Odlums Cream Flour advertisement featuring original Cream flour bag, Kerryman, 4th November 1961

Figure 60: Design for Odlums range by Talmadge Associates ca. 1963

and adapted by, unfortunately anonymous, commercial artists, many of whom worked freelance.

Some of the original designs (fig. 56 & 57) were quite basic and lacked consistency between one product and another. Like the cotton sacks before them, printing of the bags was normally done with a flexographic process using rubber stereos for the reproduction of the image. The number of colours was restricted - often a maximum of three - and tight registration of the print was difficult to achieve. It was an inexpensive process with the emphasis on quantity rather than quality.

The catalyst for change in standards of design in Ireland is often credited to the arrival in the country during the 1950s of a number of Dutch designers, many of whom had been trained by Bauhaus graduates.[13] They were to fill a void in an emerging industry that lacked the experience of working on large, international corporate accounts.[14] But it was to England that Odlums looked for inspiration for design, a move that developed the iconic imagery that is still part of the brand today.

Figure 61: Odlums in-store display ca. 1967

Figure 62: Odlums stand RDS Spring Show ca. 1965

It was the idea of the then Chairman of Odlums, Claude Odlum, to incorporate the owl symbol of the Odlums family crest (fig. 58) into the design, which is officially described in heraldic terms as:

'Gules, a chevron or between three owls affrontee proper, ducally crowned of the first, barbed and sealed gold. For crest, on a wreath of the colours, an owl affrontee proper, ducally crowned and beaked or, mantled gules doubled argent.'

In 1962 the firm of R.H. Talmadge Associates of London was commissioned to come up with new designs. Talmadge is likely to have been chosen as they were already undertaking a project to redesign the range of Jacobs biscuits. Jacobs were major customers of Odlums and with strong links between the two companies, it is probable that Gordon Lambert provided the initial introduction to Talmadge.

A 'before and after' view of the design (see fig.59 and 60) shows how they had developed over time. This 'before' image, dating from 1961, features an Odlums Cream flour pack of rudimentary design - essentially it is just text, there is no house style to distinguish it from its competitors. By contrast, the Talmadge designs brought a consistency in the use of graphics and logos across the full product range, evidence of a new professional rigour. All the designs carry the owl logo in a prominent position with the product name placed underneath; this gave a powerful on-shelf impact. A promotional leaflet produced by Talmadge states that the designs were 'enormously successful where sales rose 25 per cent after redesign.'[15] The enduring nature of this design is such that almost 50 years after its first appearance, the basic elements - the owl symbol and the Odlums logo - still remain on the products produced by the company today.

Building Brand Awareness

The retail revolution and the availability of small packs provided the manufacturer and retailer the opportunity to join forces in promoting products in store. In keeping with the motto 'Pile it high, sell it cheap', large aisle-end displays of product began to appear in the late 1960s in the new supermarket stores. Typical of these was the display for Odlums dating from c.1968 (fig.61). These displays did much to establish brand awareness and brand loyalty for local Irish products and was a critical part in the marketing programme of Odlums products. Another opportunity to showcase the company's products was through the (now defunct) annual RDS Spring Show and Industries Fair, held in May in the Society's showgrounds in Ballsbridge, Dublin. An important date on the farming and social calendar, this provided a conduit to an audience of 150,000 people, many of whom were amongst the core, rural market for flour products. Odlums maintained a stand at the Show for many years, promoting their products and offering baking and recipe advice to customers. Typical of the stand design, dating from ca. 1965, is the image pictured (fig. 62).

A product innovation that was ahead of its time was the flour 'shaker', introduced in 1964. This was aimed at consumers as a convenient alternative to the standard 3 ½ lb. bag. The flour was packed in a cardboard tube with a perforated metal top. The user was able to 'shake' out a small quantity of flour, as required. Although it was a novel concept, the price premium over the standard format was too much for it to catch on and it was withdrawn.

One other interesting marketing construct was the development of the persona of the Odlums home baking expert, Patricia Sullivan. Originally devised by Frank Sheerin in Arks, Odlums advertising agency, she became the public 'voice' of Odlums. Like her US

Figure 63: Press advertisement for Flour Shaker, Irish Independent, 18th September 1964.

counterpart, Betty Crocker, Patricia Sullivan was an imaginary figure, created, in part, to guarantee continuity in an environment where women were expected to give up work once they got married. She first featured in the Odlums Home Baking slot in the sponsored programme section on Radio Eireann at 8.45 a.m. one Tuesday in the Spring of 1961.[16]

Her weekly chat, usually about her current recipe (which was available free of charge to listeners who wrote in for it) would be an implicit advertisement for Odlums flour and its stellar qualities. Patricia Sullivan was also the 'author' of the Odlums recipe leaflets and cookery books, the first of which Odlums *Guide to Home Baking* appeared in 1963. This unassuming 40 page booklet, which was published in a print run of 100,000 copies, became one of key reference books for baking for a generation of housewives. These early recipes were actually created for Odlums by Mary Frances Keating who was the leading cookery writer at the time, penning a weekly column in the Women's Page of the *Sunday Independent* newspaper.[17]

These were the days when producers' brands were still dominant in the retail arena and Odlums were quick to realize the importance of maintaining consumer loyalty. One way of doing this was through forging links with women's groups such as the Irish Countrywoman's Association (ICA) which had been founded in 1910 and played a central role in educating women in the basics of domestic economy and other household skills.

Odlums established a demonstration programme which ran on Thursdays during the months of June, July and August. A day long visit to the mill in Portarlington was organized for local ICA groups who were bussed in for the occasion. The visit commenced with tea, followed by a laboratory and mill tour, and then lunch in the local East End hotel. The visitors then returned to the mill and were treated to a cookery demonstration presented by Odlums home baking advisor, the first of whom was Brenda Costigan (who was later the Cookery Editor for the *Sunday Independent* for many years).

As well as the 'in house' demonstrations in Portarlington, a programme of 'live' demonstrations was carried out around the country. These demonstrations were sociable affairs, outings for women who might have felt isolated in their own, often rural, areas. They were a means of communicating new ideas on cooking and baking in an era before there was wide access to TV. There was a sense of occasion to the event - this was an opportunity to invite an 'outsider' into their community.[18]

TV

Odlums were quick to spot the potential of TV and were early users of the newly established RTE service which began broadcasting in 1961. This opened up a whole new means of communicating with consumers and TV advertising became an important battleground in the bid to win over the hearts and minds of viewers. The potential audience expanded rapidly as by the mid - 1960s there were 348,000 TV sets in the Republic, amounting to 50% of all households.[19]

Television was used as a dynamic means of infusing extra life and interest both in the product and in home baking itself. In keeping with the other forms of communication, both the message and the presentation were kept simple - the packs, the owl logo and the strap line referring to the product excellence - 'It never varies' - featured prominently.

Although Ranks and Bolands were occasional users of the medium, Odlums were the major player and by 1968/9 dominated the airwaves through the use of 30 second commercials interspersed with 15 second cutdown versions. The main campaign ran from September to December with a back up campaign using 10 second slides, depending on the timing of Easter, running from March to the end of April.[20]

Perhaps perceived by some as unglamorous in its approach, it was this consistency in its message across all the media - press, radio, TV and outdoor (mainly Dublin buses) - that helped build the brand into the dominant position it still holds today.

Chapter 10:
Transportation - raw materials and finished products

A
ll of the Odlum mills, be they port or inland ones, were built close to nodal links - canal, rail and road. Prior to 1920, these first two were of prime importance with Sallins, Portarlington, Naas and St.Mullin's having direct access to water transport. The Mountmellick branch that linked Portarlington to the main section of the Grand Canal was completed in March 1831.[1] Part of the lands on which the mill in Portarlington was built was leased from the Grand Canal Co. for a term of 999 years from 1 May 1876, subject to a yearly rent of £8.[2] The mill in Portarlington also had strong rail links with the Great Southern and Western Railway Company opening a line between Dublin and Portarlington in 1847.[3]

Figure 64 : Barges on canal at Portarlington mill ca. 1920.

Canal

By the time the Portarlington mill opened in 1876, competition from the railway network was making transport by canal a less attractive proposition. By the late 1880s, a price war had broken out between the rail and canal companies in a bid to attract traffic. In an attempt to claim better terms from the canal company, Odlums stated that they had been offered a rate of 4 shillings per ton by rail, with the promise of a siding direct into the mill. The freight by water was 5 shillings, 3 pence per ton and the canal company advised that this rate could not be improved on. However, as a compromise, they suggested that if Odlums were willing to operate the barges themselves, they would be able to offer a competitive rate. This they agreed to do and for the next 60 years or so Odlums operated three boats on the canal network between Portarlington and Dublin. [4]

Initially these 42 ton boats were horse drawn with the horses stabled in a building that now adjoins the GAA grounds in Portarlington. A team of two horses was used which were rotated - as one tired, it was replaced by the second one. A man walked with the horse but he was not considered to be part of the crew.[5] Over time these boats were converted to motor power and fitted with Bolinder single cylinder, semi-diesel 15 horsepower engines which made a distinctive 'put put' sound. Odlums were one of the first companies to operate these motorized barges, designated 17B, 18B and 97B. [6*]

These boats, manned by a crew of three [7], plied their way between Dublin and Portarlington, with a cargo of wheat for the mill and, for the most part, sailing empty on the return trip. This journey took nearly a day each way to complete, about half the time as the horse-drawn barges took - but the 19 locks to be negotiated between Lucan and the Ringsend basin were a time consuming affair, irrespective of the type of boat that was being used. The grain intake in Portarlington had a capacity of 20 tons per hour and used a vertical chain system which could be lowered into the grain in the boat. This meant that a boat could be unloaded in just over 2 hours.

Over time the amount of goods carried on the Grand Canal continued to decline from a total of 226,648 tons transported in 1920 to 160, 173 tons in 1947. [8] So with falling revenues and little prospect of expansion, the Grand Canal Co. was effectively nationalized in June 1950 with the State transport company, C.I.E, taking over the operation of the canal system. As a result, the Odlum boats were taken out of commission. During the 1950s, small amounts of grain continued to by carried by barges which were now operated by C.I.E.

But with the growing importance and efficiency of carrying goods by road, the trade eventually petered out and the Mountmellick branch was closed to navigation in 1960. Within a few years, the stretch of canal that ran alongside the mill had been filled in, as part of a ring road system for the town of Portarlington. With its demise, an important part of the region's industrial and engineering history disappeared.

* The 'B' refered to bye-trader boats - i.e. boats that were operated by private operators. 17B had a steel hull and wooden deck; 18B was built in 1905 as a horse drawn barge but later fitted with an engine. In 1939, 18B was sold and replaced by 118B, built by the Ringsend Dockyard Company. It had a capacity of 45 tons and was sold in 1955 to Waterford Harbour Board.

If the canal was the preferred means of transport for bulk raw materials, it was horse power that was used for local transport of the finished products right up to the 1940s. In Portarlington, there were originally 12 drays and six horses making deliveries in the locality, as far afield as Athy, 30 km away.[9] A 'tandem' system was used with a horse and dray, with a three ton capacity in front, and a second one tethered behind. At this stage all the product was packed in sacks - a tougher hessian material for flour destined for the bakery trade and cotton for flour for delivery to the retail and wholesale trade. Weights varied considerably with the monster 224lb[10] (101kg approx.) sacks to the more manageable 4 stone (25kg approx.).

By the 1950s, there were only two drays in operation which were used to transport flour from the mill to the nearby railway station for onward delivery. By this stage, the drays were fitted with pneumatic tyres, which improved the traction and ride quality. Nevertheless, the journey involved negotiating the swing bridge over the canal. As the approach to this was on an incline, the horse had to build up a head of steam to clear the obstacle (fig. 57). The last horse to be used for this job was big and slow, which earned him the sobriquet 'Lightning'. Originally used by Johnston Mooney & O'Brien for pulling one of the last bread vans on a Dublin sales run, he was retired to live out his days on the nearby Odlums farm.

Rail

One of the ironies of transport history in Ireland, and elsewhere, is that within a short period of its completion, the canal system became obsolete.[11] The advent of the railways in Ireland with the establishment of the Dublin-Kingstown (Dun Laoghaire) line in 1834 and the rapid expansion of the network during the mid-nineteenth century offered a quicker, more flexible and often cheaper form of transportation for goods.[12]

A number of Odlums mills had direct rail links - Portarlington, for example, and Dublin and Waterford which had rail lines right into the premises. The railway network enabled the distribution of product well beyond the range of horsedrawn vehicles. Portarlington was particularly well positioned as it was on the direct Dublin - Cork route and the starting point for the branch line to Galway. Grain in sacks was delivered by rail direct into the Dublin mill from Ardee, Co. Louth up until the end of the 1960s. [13] But there were constant claims that freight rates by rail were too high, due in part to the rail companies' high overheads and seasonality of the trade.[14]

Nevertheless, considerable amounts of bagged product was shipped by rail from Portarlington to wholesale customers in the west of Ireland - amongst these were Collins of Dunmore, Co. Galway, Hannon of Ballyhaunis and Cahill of Tuam. As this transshipment predated the days of pallets and fork trucks, each bag had to be loaded and stacked by hand into the rail wagon in Portarlington and then unloaded at its destination - a slow, laborious

Figure 65: First Odlums truck on Station Road, Portarlington, with canal bridge in background ca. 1923

(and backbreaking) process. With the advent of the supermarkets and the resulting direct store deliveries by road, delivery by rail was phased out.

Road

Despite low levels of investment, road transport became increasingly important.[15] Odlums first road vehicle is believed to be an ex-British Army vehicle purchased ca. 1923. This dramatically increased the reach of the company's distribution fleet and opened up potential new sales areas.

Figure 66: Exterior of Dublin Port Mill with railway wagons ca.1936.

There were three trucks based in Portarlington with twice that number based in Portlaoise delivering to the Midlands region, Dublin and Galway. [16]

With the increasing reliability and capacity of road vehicles, the quantity of goods transported nationally on the road network increased dramatically. The number of goods vehicles increased from 26,721 in 1951 to 43,838 in 1961 - a 64% increase.[17] By 1960, the canal system was defunct, road accounted for about 80% of total ton-mileage (with the vast majority carried in trucks with a capacity over 2 tonnes) with rail accounting for the remaining 20%.[18] For Odlums, it was now possible to transport 15 tonnes of wheat from Dublin to Portarlington in approximately two hours compared to nearly a day by canal. The original vehicles, dating from the late 1950s, were quite primitive - essentially flat bed trucks with sides added to them; grain constantly seeped through the cracks!

Increased automation in the bakery business through the installation of bulk flour storage systems also changed the way in which flour was delivered to them. Odlums purchased a number of Leyland four-axle bulk flour tankers during the 1960s to supply flour to the larger bakery customers. With this higher level of throughput of flour, additional storage capacity was required - new holding bins were installed in Dublin in 1960 and Portarlington in 1965.

Initially each Odlums mill operated as a separate entity with its own salesforce and transport. In certain areas where the sales territories overlapped, there was the possibility that the company's salesforce could be competing with each other - a situation that was far from ideal.

Figure 67: Bulk flour tanker: ca. 1970 (Heart's Delight was a flour brand produced by Odlums)

As a result, in the 1970s deliveries were centralised - with Cork serving the south and west of the country and Portarlington servicing the remainder. As the delivery crews were paid 'on the clock', the system encouraged excessive overtime. This resulted in many lay-bys in the vicinity of the mills being filled with returning Odlums trucks. The driver and helper sat in the cab, delaying their return to base for as late as they could manage. Some stayed out as late as 8.00 or 9.00 p.m.

One interesting innovation during the mid 1970s was the introduction of 'swappable' bodies for the delivery trucks. This meant that loads could be made up in advance on one body during normal working hours. They were then transferred onto the delivery truck by a 'slave' vehicle overnight, leaving them ready for distribution on the following day. Although initially successful as a cost cutting exercise, the relatively small sizes of the loads and the tendency of the 'stilts' that supported the body to collapse meant that they were eventually phased out and replaced by articulated trucks.

A productivity scheme devised in the 1980s sought to address the cost structure of the transport operation. Deliveries to smaller shops were phased out and the minimum drop size increased. With its implementation, the long days came to an end with all the trucks back at base by 6.00 p.m. However, the terms that were negotiated proved so beneficial to the operatives that the wage rates skyrocketed. Employees engaged in the transport area were the highest paid group of workers and it posed a difficulty for the company to find suitable employees to work in the more skilled areas of the business, particularly in the flour mill itself.

A further rationalisation scheme saw the phasing out of the helper and a switch to one man delivery crews. All deliveries were now completed using a tractor and articulated trailer fitted with a tail lift; pallet trucks were used to transfer the loads. Despite initial misgivings as to the workability of the plan, this became the blueprint for future deliveries. But the days of owner operated fleets were numbered and the whole transport operation was outsourced (by the new owners) in 1991 and subsequently operated by independent contractors.

The Fifth Generation

All descendants of Richard Edward Odlum(1849-1924) - milling families only

FRANCIS PETER
1879-1916

Robert Ronald *(Rollo)*
1914 - 1988
m. Sheila Joughan *1920 -*

Timothy
1959 -

Nigel
1961-
*(Last family member
to work for Odlums)*

RICHARD ROSSMORE
1883-1961

Richard Douglas
1911-1992
m. Dorothy Blow *1909 - 1997*

Neila
1940 -

Joan
1947 - 2001

Michael
1951 -

LLEWLLYN DIGBY
1882-1955

Norman *1919-2007*
m. Wendy Dixon *1922-2012*

Richard *1922-2002*
m. Patricia Hogan *1933-2014*

Loftus *1929 -*
m. Dorothy Frankland *1925 -*

Caroline
1948 -

Mark
1954 -

Sally Anne
1955 -

Keith
1959 -

Johnathon
1960 -

Philip
1953 -

Stephen
1955 -
(Author)

Melanie
1960 -

ARTHUR WELLESLEY
1884-1959

Cyril
1918-1997
m. Nesta Redmond *1930-2016*

Amanda
1960 -

Jeremy
1962 -

Camilla
1963 -

Chapter 11:
New Challenges and a New Direction

Peter Odlum did not live long enough to see the fruits of the investment in modernizing the mills, as he died in March 1983, just short of his 70th birthday. In his latter years, his absences from the business became of increasing duration as he spent much of the summer on board his last yacht, M.V. Verna which was berthed in Palma, Majorca. Claude Odlum, his uncle, had predeceased him in 1979, at the great age of 94[*]. For the last decade or so of his life, Claude sported an eye patch, having lost an eye to cancer. The passing of these two individuals marked the end of the involvement of the offspring of W.P. Odlum and the dominance of this particular branch of the family in running the business. Cyril Odlum

Figure 68: Peter Odlum ca. 1980

took over the role of Chairman of Odlum Group in 1985, having already served two terms as President of IFMA in 1978-9 and 1981-2.

In terms of a legacy, Peter Odlum left behind a reinvigorated flour milling business which had benefitted from a significant amount of investment and rebuilding. Attempts to diversify into different areas were more problematic and spanned a very wide spectrum - some having direct connections with the flour business and others totally unrelated, with a distinct lack of synergy between them. These included grain and seed handling (Irish Grain), animal feed (Bestock), luggage manufacture (Travel Goods), fine china and tableware retailing (China Showrooms), motor factoring (T. & G. Aston) and fibreglass sheet manufacture (Euroglass). None of these businesses prospered and Euroglass was a disaster as the unproven manufacturing process led to a series of production issues.

[*] Claude, his wife, Doris and his youngest daughter, Mavis, are all buried in the one family plot in the Maudlings burial ground just outside Naas. Claude is reputed to have requested the Kildare Hunt to 'hunt' over his grave – a good anecdote but not one that has been confirmed!

But Peter was also aware of the challenges that flour milling in Ireland would face and was open to the possibility of selling the business. Summoned to join one of the last Board meetings that Peter attended, fifth generation members, Philip Odlum and Raymond Tilson, were advised in his parting words: 'Don't sell the business too cheap!'[1]

The flexibility shown by Odlums in their willingness to restructure their business and undertake significant new investment marked them out from their competitors. Ranks, by contrast, had invested little in the upgrading of their mills in Dublin, Cork and Limerick and were becoming increasingly inefficient and antiquated. The initial plans to close the Limerick mill had been deferred in 1975, due to local political pressure. But the crisis continued and with the business haemorrhaging money - reportedly £7,500 a day - Ranks decided to cease producing flour in Ireland and in February 1983 the mills in Dublin and Limerick were closed.[2] Ranks were determined to hold on to their market share and warned the other members of the IFMA against poaching any of their customers. Within a short period of time, all flour sold by Ranks was now produced in the UK and shipped to Ireland, reverting to a situation that had existed prior to 1930.

Despite all the efficiencies that came with the upgrading of the Odlums mills, when compared to the UK, the relative costs of production remained high. Wages, fuel and insurance costs (as they still are today) were higher in Ireland and most of the wheats used in the production of flour for the commercial bakeries had to be imported. During the 1980s there were a number of poor Irish harvests. The minutes of the 1984 AGM of the IFMA refer to a 'completely disastrous harvest and no milling wheat of any consequence (was) available for purchase by the industry'. The market was effectively decontrolled in 1985 with the abolition of the National Prices Commission although its role was becoming increasingly irrelevant with the downward pressure on prices being imposed by ever increasing levels of imports of flour.

In February 1987, for the first time in its history, a non-family member, Patrick McEvilly was appointed as Chief Executive of the company. Formerly, Chief Executive of Bord na Mona, he introduced a programme of planning and financial controls that had previously been lacking and a new sense of direction and purpose. A complete strategic evaluation of the business was undertaken and a decision was made to wind down the Bestock animal feed business with the closure of the feed mills in Dublin, Sligo and Sallins. The Board was also strengthened by the addition of Niall McCarthy of the Goodalls food company who was brought in as a non-executive Director to add a new marketing dimension to the business.

The profile of the commercial bakeries was also changing. The traditional bakeries in Dublin such as Johnston Mooney and O'Brien, Bolands and Mother's Pride, which were highly unionized, were facing calls for reduced working hours and productivity payments for the installation of new equipment. By contrast, in the 1970s new entrants appeared, epitomized by Joseph Brennan Bakeries, who remained outside the union environment. As such, they were able to exploit the restriction on night baking imposed by the Night Work in Bakeries Act (1936) and supply bread that was much fresher than that available from its competitors, particularly on a Monday. Deliveries were undertaken by owner drivers, as opposed to salaried drivers and 'van boys' which dramatically reduced distribution costs. Capital costs also remained low due to the availability of second hand bakery equipment imported from the UK from bakeries that were either upgrading or closing down there. Over time, these new entrants took an increasing share of the bread market, which not only affected the traditional bakeries' profit margins but also reduced the amount of flour that the millers were able to sell into their own bakeries.

By the mid 1980s, profit margins had been seriously eroded within the operating company, Odlum Group Ltd. and it posted a loss of over £1 million in 1984.[3] A series of rationalization programmes within the Johnston Mooney & O'Brien bakery helped stem these losses for a couple of years. The purchase by Odlums of the Butterkrust bakery operation from the receiver in 1987 was an attempt to secure its flour business and expand the bakery arm to compete with the aggressive newcomers such as Brennans and Pat the Baker.

But the arrival of another low cost operator in Dublin market effectively delivered the *coup de grace* to the business. A new bakery in Ballyfermot, operated by Nevilles, but bankrolled by the Dunne supermarket family, opened in early 1989. Overnight the price of a 800g sliced loaf fell from a standard 79p to 35p, produced by a non-union bakery employing fewer than 40 employees and selling only two products – a white and brown sliced loaf. Against this Johnston Mooney & O'Brien operated from a large site that was unsuited to modern production techniques, had an extensive product range and employed a workforce in excess of 480. Losses quickly became unsustainable and the company was placed in voluntary liquidation on 27 February 1989, marking the end of more than 150 years baking activity on the Ballsbridge site. Ironically, the bakery brands were purchased by a Brennans/Readibake combine, together with the former Butterkrust bakery premises in Finglas, Dublin. As part of the terms of sale, an agreement to supply flour to the Finglas bakery was put in place

The year 1989 also witnessed the demise of the IFMA, which had been founded 87 years previously. Following the merging of Bolands (now part of I.A.W.S), Dock Milling and S. & A.G. Davis businesses in 1988, the Association effectively had only two members. In November 1989 Bolands withdrew, leaving Odlums as the only surviving member. The Association was wound up on the final day of that year. Norman Odlum had the dubious honour of being the last President, bringing to an end an association that Odlums had with IFMA since its inception.*

Having been Company Secretary since 1986, Philip Odlum was appointed to the Board

* On a more positive note Norman Odlum was elected First Vice President of the 'Groupement' of the Milling Associations of the E.E.C. (later Association of European Millers) in 1984 and President in 1987 - the only time this position has been held by an Irishman.

of Odlum Group in January 1989 - the first of the fifth generation (and last ever) member to be appointed to the position. There was intensive activity during the summer months examining options to put the flour milling business on a more secure footing. Among those considered were a merger with Bolands; an alternative was reversing the combined milling interests of Odlums and Andrews into R. & H. Hall. Ironically, the divestiture of its baking arm made the Odlums milling business more attractive as a takeover target. The state owned Irish Sugar Company (of which Algernon had been a Chairman and Director) under the direction of Chris Comerford, was looking to expand its business into new areas and viewed the Odlum milling business as an attractive prospect.

With a generous purchase price on offer, combined with an uncertain future and a family shareholding that was now widely dispersed across the globe, the difficult decision to sell was made. The Irish Sugar Company took a 50% interest in Odlum Group in November 1989 for £17.6m, appointing Comerford as the new Chairman, a majority of the Directors and taking overall management control. The remaining 50% was sold in April 1991, when Irish Sugar was privatized and became the publicly quoted company, Greencore.

This brought to a close more than 125 years of Odlums ownership of the milling business that bears its name. The Maryborough / Portlaoise mill was demolished in August 1990, bringing to an end a material presence that the Odlum family had with the town since 1865. Sadly, there is no marker to denote the location of the mill which was once a focal point of the town.

In 1978 the Shackelton mill in Lucan had been taken over by Roma Foods and converted to make flour for pasta products *; it eventually closed in November 1998. The Davis mill in Enniscorthy closed in 1990 as did Milford Flour Mills and The Dock Milling Company ceased production in 1994.[4] By the close of the twentieth century, there were only six flour mills in operation on the island of Ireland - the three Odlums mills and Bolands in the Republic of Ireland and Andrews and Neil's (part of ABF plc) in Northern Ireland.

* Richard (Dick) Shackelton (1916-2000) retired from the mill on 31st. December 1991. This marked the end of the involvement of the Shackelton family in flour milling, bringing to a close a tradition which had started in ca. 1776 in Ballytore, Co. Kildare.

Epilogue

Following the original sale of the business in 1991, a further series of sales and mergers followed, with each transaction resulting in a diminution of the company in terms of its importance and profile. Greencore sold out to Origin (originally part of I.A.W.S) in 2007 with Valeo Foods taking ownership of Odlums in September 2010. A series of mill closures also took place during this period - Cork closed in 2009, Dublin in 2012 and the oatmeal plant in Sallins finally ceased production in December 2013. This left just one flour mill operating in the Republic of Ireland - the Odlums mill in Portarlington, managed by Nigel Odlum, the last of the family members working in the business. This mill is the sole survivor of an industry that, together with sugar production, were once a core plank of Fianna Fáil's early policy of self-sufficiency and central to the country's wellbeing and development. Of *Irish Sugar*, former owner of Odlums, nothing survives - with the last remaining factory in Mallow closed down in May 2006 and the site cleared.

One final thought; if all the new investment that took place in the 1960s and 1970s had been concentrated on building a single new large-scale mill in Dublin, would the business have faced a different future and possibly remained in family ownership? Or, as is the case today, is it the brand that is important (take Nike as a case in point) and where the product is made is irrelevant? If that holds sway, then there is little future for the flour milling industry in Ireland.

NOTES:

TERMINOLOGY

Maryborough/Portlaoise: I have used the name Maryborough up to 1930 approx. This was the name that appeared in newspaper articles relating to the business as well as the name used by Odlums in their publicity material, stationery etc.

Sack : traditionally flour mill capacity was measured in sacks per hour of flour. One sack equates to 280lb of flour (8 sacks = 1 imperial tonne/2240lbs).

Now mill capacity is measured in tons of wheat milled per 24-hour day; a 50 sack flour mill processes approx. 215 tons of wheat per hour

ABBREVIATIONS

D.G.: archive of Rev. Douglas Graham

LLO: Loftus Odlum notes and memoirs

RRO: archive of Rollo Odlum

IFMA: Irish Flour Millers Association

REFERENCES:

Chapter 1: The Four Brothers

1. Hogg, (2002), p. vi
2. Deed 836.96.560431, dated 18 April 1828
3. Hogg, (2002), p. 72
4. Douglas Graham papers
5. Grave witnessed by Capt. W.J. Odlum on 28th. September 1920
6. Douglas Graham (D.G.) papers
7. Inventory W.P. Odlum - correspondence between A. McClure and A. A. Odlum, 27 February 1934
8.   D. G. papers
9.   Ditto
10. Valuation Book No. 5.1306
11. Deed No. 1853.25.79, dated 1 September 1853
12. Information from Richard's son, Richard William Odlum to William Henry Odlum of Ardmore, Bray, Co. Wicklow in 1927; D.G. papers
13. Valuation Book No. 5.1306
14. D. G. papers
15. *The Miller,* Obituary, William Podger, 11 August 1901
16. Correspondence between Richard Odlum and his son.
17. Information from Richard's son, Richard William Odlum to William Henry Odlum in 1927; D.G. papers
18. Heston and Isleworth: *Mills', A History of the County of Middlesex: Volume 3: Shepperton,*

Staines, Stanwell, Sunbury, Teddington, Heston and Isleworth, Twickenham, Cowley, Cranford, West Drayton, Greenford, Hanwell, Harefield and Harlington (1962), pp. 112-114. URL: http://www.british-history.ac.uk/report.aspx?compid=22278 Date accessed: 06 November 2013.
19. Correspondence between Muriel Falkiner and Douglas Graham, 20 February 1978
20. Correspondence with Rev. Michael Odlum

Chapter 2. Building Blocks

1. Goodbody, M. (2011), p. 41
2. Inventory W.P. Odlum - correspondence between A. McClure and A. A. Odlum, 27 February 1934.
3. Cullen, L.M. (2003). Eighteenth-Century Flour Milling in Ireland in Bielenberg, A. (ed), *Irish Flour Milling - A History 600-2000*, pp. 39-58.
4. Correspondence between Horace Turpin, Solicitors and R.R. Odlum, 17 December 1960
5. William Podger obituary - The Miller, 11 August 1901
6. Author's interview with Muriel Falkiner, 26 June 1990D.G. papers
7. Undated interview between D.G. and Muriel Falkiner
8. ditto
9. ditto
10. D.G. papers
11. Undated interview between D.G and Muriel Falkiner
12. ditto
13. ditto
14. Correspondence between Stokes Bros and W P & R Odlum - D.G. collection
15. Kilkenny County Council, 2009,Heritage Audit of the Northern River Nore: an Action Plan of the Draft Kilkenny Heritage Plan 2007-201, Volume 2, Built Heritage Inventory http://www.kilkennycoco.ie/resources/eng/Services/Heritage/Nore_Heritage_Audit/light/Vol_2_RNHA_light.pdf
16. *Leinster Express* -100 Years ago this week, 26 August 1976
17. Jones, G. (2003), The Introduction and Establishment of Roller Milling in Ireland in Bielenberg, A. (ed), *Irish Flour Milling - A History 600-2000*, pp. 106-32
18. Bielenberg. A. (2003). A survey of Irish Flour Milling, 1801-1922 in Bielenberg, A. (ed), *Irish Flour Milling - A History 600-2000*, pp. 59-87.
19. R.R. Odlum papers 16 December 1960
20. Bielenberg. A. (2003) p. 68
21. Jones, G. (2003) p.127
22. Odlum & Pemberton, misc. papers relating to Leinster Mills, Co. Kildare. Hoey & Denning Box 37 & 38 cases N-O inc. T5948-T5958. National Archives, Dublin D.G. papers
23. Despite strong anecdotal evidence, I was unable to find confirmation of this through court records. So without this, it must remain conjecture.
24. R.R. Odlum papers, 16 December 1960

25. *The Miller*, 1 March 1948, front cover
26. Simon advertisement from *The Miller*, January 1890
27. *The Miller*, July 5 1886, p. 179
28. *The Miller*, July 4 1887, p. 181
29. D.G. papers
30. William Odlum obituary - *The Miller*, Vol. VII, 3 October 1881, p.608
31. Ditto
32. R.R.O. papers
33. D.G. papers
34. Bielenberg, A. (2003) p.86

Chapter 3: A Growing Family
1. Author's interview with Muriel Falkiner, 26 June 1990
2. Ditto
3. Correspondence with Hazel Falkiner (daughter of Muriel Falkiner) 5 July 1990
4. Illustrated address given to Algernon Odlum on the occasion of his wedding - property of Mrs. C. Hamilton
5. Address given on Richard Edward (Ross) Odlum's birth certificate 12 December 1883
6. Census of Ireland 1901
7. Census of Ireland 1911
8. *Leinster Express*, May 1899
9. *The Miller*, Vol. XXV, 5 June 1889, p. 232
10. Interview with Loftus Odlum (LLO), 2 December 2013
11. *The Miller*, Vol. XXXVI, 6 June 1910, p.216
12. *The Miller*, 6 December 1909, p. 647
13. R.R. Odlum notes
14. *Milling*, 23 December 1911, p. 620

Chapter 4: The Third Generation
1. *Milling*, 23 December 1911
2. Author's interview with Muriel Falkiner, 26 June 1990
3. ditto
4. LLO
5. LLO
6. Library & Archives Canada: Soldiers of the First World War - CEF, www.collectionscanda.gc.ca
7. National Archives: Census of Ireland 1911
8. http://www.gracesguide.co.uk/Eadie_Manufacturing_Co
9. Unattributed 1912 newspaper article - DG papers
10. ditto

11. van Esbeck, E., (1974). *One Hundred Years of Irish Rugby*. Dublin. Gill & Macmillan. p.199
12. Unattributed 1913 newspaper article - DG papers
13. Goodbody, M. (2011), p. 396
14. Whelan, E. (2012) p.15
15. now in author's possession

Chapter 5: An Industry under Threat
1. Bielenberg, (2003), p. 83
2. Takei, (2003), p. 135
3. *Milling*, 25 October 1924, p. LVI
4. Larmour, (2009), p. 8
5. *Milling*, 25 October 1924, p. XXXIX
6. *Milling*, 25 October 1924, p. XLVII
7. Riordan, (1920), p. 275
8. *Irish Times*, 13 January 1906, p.13
9. Daly, (1992), p. 23
10. Takei, (2003), p. 138
11. Whelan, (2012), p. 17
12. Goodbody, M. , (2011), p. 443
13. Niall Higgins archive
14. IFMA minutes, National Archive: DUB/128/B/2/9
15. Daly, (1992), p. 50

Chapter 6: An improving landscape
1. Daly, (1992), p.62
2. Takei, (2003), p.141
3. Burls, (1958), p.168
4. Takei, (2003), p.142
5. Takei, (2003), p. 153
6. ditto
7. *Milling*, 22 April 1933
8. R.R. Odlum notes
9. *The Miller*, 15 January 1934, p.79
10. *Milling*, September 7 1929, p.259
11. *Milling*, 8 July 1933
12. Takei, (2003), p. 142
13. Takei, (2003), p. 146
14. Takei, (2003), p. 152
15. Takei, (1998), p. 296

16. Correspondence with Elizabeth Richmond 22 March 2014
17. Interview with Elizabeth Richmond 14 February 2014
18. This was the Abbey Church, Ferrybank, Waterford, which was closeby to Sion Hill and now in somewhat parlous condition. Ross acted as Hon. Treasurer for many years. Ross and Nora are buried there along with daughter, Sheila Thomas and her husband, Harold.
19. *Interview with Elizabeth Richmond*, 14 February 2014
20. Ross Odlum obituary - *Irish Times,* 24 December 1961
21. Interview with Elizabeth Richmond, 14 February 2014
22. Passenger lists from www.ancestry.co.uk
23. Freemasons Hall, Molesworth Street, Dublin records
24. Correspondence between Peter Odlum and J. Sedgwick & Co., 3 October 1951
25. Kirwan J. & Bellewstown Heritage Group, 2013, p. 201
26. Interview with Clare Hamilton, 21 January 2014

Chapter 7: Fourth Generation

1. Memorandum and Articles of Association of W.P. & R. Odlum Ltd.
2. IFMA records National Archives, Dublin.
3. LLO
4. LLO
5. LLO
6. Correspondence with Mark Odlum (son), May 2014
7. *Milling,* Vol LXXIX, 21 June 1948, p. 538
8. RRO
9. Delaney (1973), p. 205
10. Odlum R., (1991), Post War Musings - The Odlum Formula II Frazer Nash in *Chain Gang Gazette,* April 1991
11. Wikipedia, 1955 24 Hours of Le Mans, http://en.wikipedia.org/wiki/1955_24_Hours_of_Le_Mans
12. Peter Odlum succeded his uncle, Ninian Falkiner, as Commodore. Ninian was married to Muriel Odlum, youngest daughter of W.P. and Emma Odlum. Peter was a generous benefactor to the Royal Irish Yacht Club. The pair of chandeliers in the drawing room were purchased through a bequest he made. He was also responsible for the repurchase of two silver antique claret jugs which had originally been presented to the Royal Irish by the Duchess of Kent as Regatta prizes and later sold out of the Club.
13. Boylan (1994), p. 124
14. As described by his future wife, Nesta Odlum, née Redmond
15. RRO notes

Chapter 8: Consolidation and Rationalization

1. Campion, N., (2003), pp. 156-7
2. *Milling,* 28 January 1966, p. 92.
3. Campion, (2003), p.156
4. Douglas and Dorothy Odlum left the mill house at St. Mullin's and moved to Bridgetown, Co. Wexford. The mill house, unfortunately, fell into disrepair and is now totally derelict
5. IFMA - National Archive: DUB/128/B/2/44
6. RRO
7. Campion, (2003) p. 159
8. RRO
9. *Milling,* 1 April 1960, p. 365
10. RRO
11. Ever one with an eye for a bargain, in 1921 Claude Odlum had purchased a complete 7-sack plant secondhand from Carrs, Silloth in Cumbria and installed it in the Naas mill. With the exception of a change to a pneumatic handling system which was installed in 1957, the mill was virtually unchanged at the time of its closure in 1978.
12. Promotional brochure produced by MIAG - 'W.P. &R. Odlum Ltd. Dublin - Ready to join the Common Market', October 1972
13. LLO
14. IFMA - National Archive (DUB/128/B/2/57)
15. *Irish Press,* 14 April 1975

Chapter 9: Marketing and Material Culture

1. Campion, (2002)
2. Stewart, (1965), p. 25
3. IFMA minutes
4. Oram, (1986), p.295
5. Shirlow, (1997), p. 88
6. Campion, (2003), p. 156
7. Brown, (2002), p. 230
8. Brown, (2002), p. 231
9. Farmar, (2010), p. 203
10. Interviews with L.Odlum and N. Higgins, MD of Dock Milling
11. Interviews with L. Odlum and G. Conway: 30 April 2013
12. Oram, (1986), p.60
13. The Bauhaus was a design school established in Germany post-WW1 which espoused Modernism in its teaching philosophy.
14. King, (2011), p.167
15. R.H. Talmadge Associates: *Designers at Work*

16. Frank Sheerin - Arks and the Odlums Owls, printed in *Development Magazine,* Spring 1966
17. Interview with Brenda Costigan, 27 September 2012
18. ditto
19. King & Sisson, (2011), p.157
20. Interview with Niall Hanna, 28 August 2012

Chapter 10: Transport

1. Laois County Council, (2008), p.6
2. Correspondence between RRO and Howard Jones, Mayne & Knapp, 13 December 1960
3. Laois County Council, 2008, p.11
4. Delany, (1973), p. 186
5. Interview between Loftus Odlum and Michael McNamara (ex-mill worker, Portarlington) - 8 January 1988
6. Laois County Council, 2008, p.16
7. This was reduced to 2 men in 1952
8. Delaney, (1973), p. 208
9. Interview between Loftus Odlum and Edward (Ned) Downey (ex-mill worker, Portarlington) - December 1989.
10. The 224lb, 98lb and 70lb bags were withdrawn from use in all counties except Donegal in March 1934: IFMA minutes
11. The Grand Canal from Dublin to the Shannon was completed in 1804; the branch lines to Kilbeggan, Mountmellick and Ballinalsoe were open by 1836. The Royal Canal was completed in 1817 (Cullen, 1972, p. 122)
12. Delany, (1973), p. 233
13. Interview with David Micks, 18 June 2014
14. Cullen, (1972), 142-144
15. Reynolds, (1962), p.1
16. LLO
17. Reynolds, (1962), p.3
18. Reynolds, (1962), p. 10

Chapter 11: New Challenges and a New Direction

1. Interview with Philip Odlum
2. Whelan, (2012), p. 134
3. Odlum Group Ltd. annual accounts, 1984
4. Campion, (2003), p.175

BIBLIOGRAPHY
Periodicals & pamphlets
Henry Simon Ltd. occasional Letter. Number 243, October 1957; Number 251, November 1960
The Miller, London
Milling, Turret Press, London
Free State Farmer, November 1936.
Business and Finance: Vol. 1 No. 1 - 18 September 1964 - 30 December 1966
Vol. 13, No. 16 - Vol. 15, No. 15. 1977-8

PRINTED BOOKS
BIELEBERG, A. (ed), (2003). *Irish Flour Milling - a History 600-2000.* Dublin: Lilliput Press.
BOYLAN, H., (1994). *White Sails Crowding - a history of the Royal Irish Yacht Club.*
Dublin: A. & A. Farmar.
BURLS, J. (ed.) (1958). *Nine Generations : a history of the Andrews family, millers of Comber.*
Isaac Andrews.
CAMPION, N. (2010). Forty-four - four. *Grist to the Mill -Newsletter of the Irish Mills and Millers.*
Spring 2010. Issue 17, p. 14-16.
CAMPION, N. 2003. *Irish Flour Milling since the Second World War* in BIELEBERG, A. (ed), Irish
Flour Milling - a History 600-2000. Dublin: Lilliput Press. pp. 153-77.
CULLEN, L.M., (1972) *An Economic History of Ireland since 1660.* London: B.T. Batsford Ltd.
DALY, M. (1992) I*ndustrial Development and Irish National Identity 1922-1939.* Syracuse: Syracuse
University Press.
DELANEY, R. (1973). *The Grand Canal of Ireland.* Newton Abbot: David & Charles
GOODBODY, M. (2011). *The Goodbodys - Millers, Merchants and Manufacturers.* Dublin: Ashfield Press.
GRIBBON, H.D. (1996) *Economic and Social History 1850-1921 in* VAUGHAN. W.E. (ed) Ireland
under the Union, II 1870-1921, Vol. VI, Chapter XII, pp. 260-356
HOGG, W., (2000), *The Millers & the Mills of Ireland of about 1850,* Dublin: William Hogg.
HOLLANDER, J. (2007) *Coloured political lithographs as Irish propaganda: warrior artists and the
battle for home rule, 1879-1886. Lewiston,* N.Y. ; Lampeter : Edwin Mellen Press
KIRWAN, J. & Bellewstown Heritage Group, (2013), *Almost 300 years of racing at Bellewstown,
Bellewstown Heritage Group.*
KING, L and SISSON, E. (eds.) (2011), *Ireland: Design and Visual Culture: Negotiating Modernity,
1922-1992. Cork:* Cork University Press.
LAOIS COUNTY COUNCIL, (2008), *The Mountmellick Canal*
LARMOUR, P. (2009) *Free State Architecture - Modern Movement Architecture in Ireland, 1922-1949.
Kinsale:* Gandon Editions.
MILLARD, J. (1996) Never a Dull Moment. Cambridge. Silent Books.
MORRIS, E. (2005) *Our Own Devices: National Symbols and Political Conflict in Twentieth*-Century
Ireland. Dublin: Irish Academic Press

MUNCK, R. (1993) *The Irish Economy - Results and Prospects.* London: Pluto Press.

O'BRIEN, J. (2013) *As times go by - photographs and memories.* Arderin Publishing Company. (p. 56)

O'BRIEN, J. & FENNELLY, T (1996) *Glimpses of Portlaoise : A Pictorial Parade - People, Places, Events.* Portlaoise: Leinster Express.

REYNOLDS, D.J. (1962) *Inland Transport in Ireland: A Factual Survey,* Paper No. 10. Dublin: ERSI

RIORDAN, E.J. (1920) *Modern Irish Trade and Industry.* London: Methuen & Co. Ltd.

STEWART, M. (1965). *Goodbodys of Clara*: 1865-1965. London: Neame

TAKEI, A. (2003). Political Economy of the Irish Flour Milling Industry in BIELEBERG, A. (ed), *Irish Flour Milling - a History 600-2000.* Dublin: Lilliput Press. pp. 131-151.

WHELAN, E. *(2012), Ranks Mills - The Industrial Heart of Limerick City.* Limerick: Brunswick Press.

WEB BASED SOURCES:

Laois County Council, 2005, Mills of Co. Laois: An Industrial Heritage Survey Part 2: Site inventory, http://www.laois.ie/YourCouncil/Publications/Heritage/FileDownload,1781,en.pdf

Kilkenny Co. Council http://www.kilkennycoco.ie/resources/eng/Services/Heritage/Nore_Heritage_Audit/light/Vol_2_RNHA_light.pdf

UNPUBLISHED PAPERS:

CAMPION, N. (2002) Packaging and Branding. Unpublished draft for Irish Flour Milling: A History 600-2000

LAMBERT, G. (1963) 'Industrial Design in Advertising & Packaging in Ireland' Association of Advertisers in Ireland, pp.1-11

THESES

TAKEI, A. (1998) Business and Government in the Irish Free State: The Case of the Irish Flour Milling Industry 1922-1945. Ph.D., University of Dublin

COMPANY RECORDS

Irish Flour Millers Association: Minutes of meetings
National Archives, Dublin: DUB 128/B/1/1: 16 January 1934- 17 December 1941; Dub 128/B/1/2 Jan 1942-November 1947;Dub 128/B/1/3 :12 December 1947- June 1953; DUB128/B/1/14-15
AGM yearbooks: DUB/128/B/21-68

ODLUM & PEMBERTON, ODLUMS COMPANY RECORDS

National Archives, Dublin: DUB 128/A/1; DUB 128/A/2; DUB 128/A/3; DUB 128/A/4

APPENDICES:

Appendix A:

Principal Flour Milling Firms in Ireland, 1918 (see map p. 40)

1. Isaac Andrews and Sons, Belfast Mills, Belfast
2. R. Ardagh, Portlaw, Waterford.
3. Bannatyne (James) and Sons, Limerick
4. Bennett and Co., Clonakilty, Co. Cork
5. Bolands Ltd., Ringsend, Dublin
6. Brown and Crosthwait, Bagnelstown, Co. Carlow
7. Brown (Walter) and Co., Hanover Street, Dublin
8. Thos Comerford (J.) and Sons, Rathdrum, Co. Wicklow
9. North City Mills, Glasnevin, Dublin
10. Davis. S and A.G., St. John's Mill, Enniscorthy, Co. Wexford
11. Dock Milling Co. Ltd., Barrow Street, Dublin
12. Furlong (John) and Sons Ltd., Lapp's Quay and Marina Mills, Cork
13. Fogarty, Owen, Aughrim, Co. Wicklow
14. S. Gilliland & Sons, Rock Mills, Londonderry.
15. Glynn (M.) and Son, Kilrush, Co. Clare
16. Going and Smith, Cahir, Co. Tipperary
17. Goodbody, M.&J. and L., Clara, Co. Offaly
18. Hallinan (T) and Sons Ltd., Midleton, Co. Cork and Fermoy, Co. Cork
19. Hannon (H) and Sons, Ardreigh Mills, Athy, Co. Kildare
20. Howard Bros., Crookstown, Co. Cork
21. Hughes, Dickson & Co. Ltd., Belfast
22. Halligan, John, Ushers Island, Dublin
23. Johnston, Mooney and O'Brien Ltd., Clonliffe Mills, Dublin
24. Martin Maguire, Limerick.
25. R. Morton & Co., Ballymena, Co. Antrim
26. MacMullan (W.J.) and Sons Ltd., George's Quay, Cork
27. Mosse, W.H., Bennett's Bridge, Co. Kilkenny
28. James Neil, Reliable Flour Mills, Belfast.
29. Odlum and Odlum, Naas, Co. Kildare
30. Odlum, W.P & R., Maryborough, Portarlington and St.Mullin's,.
31. Oliver, W.R., Buttevant and Mallow, Co. Cork
32. Palmer (Thomas) and Co., Galway
33. Pollexfen (W. and G.T.) and Co. Ltd, Sligo
34. Pilsworth, Robert, Grennan Mills, Thomastown, Co. Kilkenny
35. R. Perry & Co., Belmont, Co. Offaly.
36. Russell (John) and Sons, Newtown Perry Milles and Mallow St. Mills (Limerick)

37. Howard Rowe, Wexford

38. Shackleton (E) and Sons, Moone and Barrow Mills, Carlow

39. Shackleton (G) and Sons Ltd; Lucan ,Co. Dublin and Straffan, Co. Kildare

40. Shaw (George) and Sons, John Street, Cork

41. John Spicer Ltd; Boyne and Blackwater Mills, Navan, Co. Meath

42. T.D. Thomas Ltd; Bridge Mills, Castletownroche, Co. Cork

43. Victoria Milling Company, Derry

44. J and R Webb, Mallow, Co. Carlow

APPENDIX B:

Claude Odlum : Racehorses and Results

Year	No. of Races	Wins	Placed (2nd, 3rd , 4th)
War Flour: br g by Spook - Divine Flower (trained by Mr. Trench)			
1918	9	1	3
1919	1	0	0
1920	1	0	1
1921	1	0	1
1923	6	4	2 (trained by Mr. Walker)
1924	5	1	2
1926	10	1	5 (trained by owner?)
1927	7	0	4
Morganol: b g by Mor Gandale - Solano (trained by Mr. Trench)			
1919	4	0	0
1920	1	0	0
1921	1	0	0
Tara: b g by Desmond - Darling Clara (trained by Mr. Trench)			
1918	2	1	0
1919	7	2	3
1920	9	1	4
1921	4	2	1

Year	No. of Races	Wins	Placed (2nd, 3rd, 4th)
Tony Boy: br g by Count Anthony - Ladoga (trained by owner?)			
1927	6	2	2
1928	4	0	1
1929	9	5	3 (trained by Mr. Arnold)
1930	4	2	0
1932	5	0	2 (trained by Mr. J. Dawson)
1933	3	0	0
La Guerre: br f by Cri de Guerre - Lagonda (trained by Mr. Blake)			
1934	2	0	1
1935	8	0	2 (trained by Mr. Jas Murphy)
1938	3	0	0 (trained by Mr. Osborne)
Tolago: b c by Tolgus - Lagonda (trained by Mr. Blake)			
1940	3	1	0
1941	5	0	1
1942	11	2	2
Wily Trout: ch c by Le Sage - Luggeen (trained by Mr. C.L. Weld)			
1962	3	0	0
1963	8	3	4
1964	5	0	3
1965	12	0	4

Wily Trout was probably Claude Odlum's most successful horse. Trained to run on the flat, it was due to run in the Irish Sweeps Derby in 1963 but was withdrawn shortly before the race. It went on to win the Desmond Stakes at the Curragh in August, ran in the Irish St. Leger in September and was entered for a race in Kempton in October which, unfortunately, was rained off.

W.P. & R.O. HOLDINGS

The history of the Holding Company dates back to the time of the final W.P. and R. Odlum Partnership agreement amongst the family members in February 1951. At this stage there were 15 partners sharing the original capital of the partnership and the profits in the following proportions:

Claude Odlum	1/4
Algernon Odlum	1/8
Peter Odlum	1/8
Arthur Odlum	1/16
Cyril Odlum	1/32
Kenneth Odlum	1/32
Digby Odlum	1/16
Norman Odlum	1/64
Perry Odlum	1/64
Richard Odlum	1/64
Loftus Odlum	1/64
Richard Rossmore Odlum	1/16
Douglas Odlum	1/16
Rollo Odlum	1/16
Cecil Tilson	1/16

It was generally accepted that the Partnership format was very unwieldy, particularly with the numbers of partners involved, but there were also concerns regarding liability for death duties and other taxes.

As a result, it was agreed to change the company structure and create a private unlimited company, W.P. & R.O. Holdings, which would acquire all the assets of the W.P. & R. Odlum Partnership which comprised shares in companies (including the milling company, W.P. & R. Odlum Ltd.), investments quoted on the Stock Exchange and farms with an approximate value of £1m. The company was incorporated on 24 March 1952 with a share capital of £800,000 made up of 400,000 5% Cumulative Preference Shares of £1 each and 400,000 Ordinary Shares of £1 each. In 1962, the share capital was increased to £1,200,000 through the issuing of a new class of 'A' share. This move was to prove contentious in later years.

We have already detailed (Chapter 7) the purchase in 1956 of the Johnston Mooney & O'Brien Ltd. bakery business. This was actually purchased in the first instance by W.P. & R.O. Holdings. In 1963 a new company, J.M. & O'B (Realization) Ltd. was formed with a capital of

£750,000 and the assets of the old company, Johnston Mooney & O'Brien Ltd., were sold to the Realization company which was subsequently liquidated. Its shareholders received £1.20 for every share held plus 1.2m shares in the new company.

In 1972 Johnston Mooney & O'Brien Ltd. made a bonus issue of 750,000 shares bringing the total share capital up to 1.5m shares of £1 each. This company was subsequently sold to Odlum Group Ltd. netting the sum of £2.5m for W.P. & R.O. shareholders.

The early Board meetings used to take place in the Board Room in the mill in Portlaoise. Presided over by Claude Odlum, who remained as Chairman into his nineties, these were formal affairs. Information flow was tightly regulated and tended to be in one direction only - from Board to shareholder. Copies of the accounts were handed out to those present in the gloomy room for a circumspect review, before they were gathered up again at the end of the meeting. There appeared to be a concern that the information might somehow leak out to the general public.

By the late 1980s conditions within the flour milling business were becoming increasingly difficult, with an ever rising flow of cheaper flour imports coming into the country. The decision to close the Johnston Mooney and O'Brien bakery business in 1989 and a reduction in the animal feed business meant that W.P. & R.O. Holdings was becoming increasingly reliant on the flour milling business for most of its income stream and there were inherent risks in this strategy.

One move that was to have a profound effect on the professional management of the company was the decision to appoint outside directors with financial and fund management experience. The first of these was Philip Jacob, who joined the Board in November 1988, becoming Chairman in the following year. This was the first time that a non-family member had acted as Chairman of the company. This had the significant advantage in that change could be implemented much more quickly; there were now no conflicts of interest and individual family interests to protect. (Philip Jacob retired in 2000 and was replaced by William (Billy) McCann.)

A committee was appointed by the Board to determine options open to the company. A search for a suitable partner was initiated and an offer by Irish Sugar to purchase the assets of Odlum Group Ltd. (in which W.P. & R.O. Holdings had a 64% shareholding) was agreed to in November 1989. The first 14% of the company was sold in March 1990 and the remaining 50% in April 1991 to Greencore plc which was the new holding company for the former state owned enterprises that included Irish Sugar and Erin Foods.

Consideration was as follows:	£
Payment for 14% Odlum Group Ltd. March 1990	4.93m.
Payment for remaining 50% April 1991	11.66m.
Plus 5,069,366 shares in Greencore at issue price of £2.30	11.66m.

This put a total valuation on the company of £40.92m. For a business that was only making £2m. in profit a year this was quite a remarkable deal. So for the first time since the original partnership was formed nearly 120 years previously, the family holding company would now not derive any income directly from flour milling.

Over a period from 1952, a series of bonus 'A' shares were issued. So by 1991 there were a total of 2,261,935 'A' non-voting shares and the original 400,000 Ordinary voting shares. Ordinary and 'A' shareholders were entitled to the same percentage dividend on the nominal amount of shares which meant that 'A' shareholders in total received a much greater dividend income than the Ordinary shareholders. A further anomaly was that the 'A' shareholders were not entitled to any surplus assets in a winding up situation.

MEELICK HOLDINGS

An attempt to resolve some of the anomalies between the different type of shareholders was put in place through the formation of Meelick Holdings.

The company was formed in January 1992 when Meelick Holdings acquired all the issued share capital of W.P.&R.O. Holdings. Holders of Ordinary shares in W.P.&R.O Holdings * were given two £1 Ordinary shares and one £1 'B' share in Meelick Holdings, plus 40p in cash for every two Ordinary shares in W.P.&R.O Holdings they held.

For owners of W.P&R.O. Holdings 'A' shares, for every two 'A' shares in the company, they received two £1 'A' shares and one £1 'B' share in Meelick Holdings plus 40p in cash. 'A' shareholders were now for the first time permitted to vote and to participate along with the Ordinary shareholders in any surplus assets in the event of the company being wound up.

The new Meelick 'A' shares remained the more valued asset as the dividend was set at 30 times the rate of the Ordinary share.

HUTTONREAD

The situation regarding the relative values of the 'A' and Ordinary shares was finally resolved with the formation of a new company, Huttonread•, in June 2000. Huttonread took over all the assets of Meelick. The offer from Huttonread was 1 Ordinary share of IR£1 each in the new company for each Ordinary share of IR£1 in Meelick. The 'A' shares were finally bought out with holders of each 'A' share in Meelick receiving 2.4 Ordinary shares of IR£1 each in Huttonread, or IR£10.50 in cash or IR£10.50 nominal of 6% Redeemable Unsecured Loan Stock 2015 in Huttonread (or a combination of any two or more).

---

* In September 1991, each W.P.&R.O. Holdings £1 Ordinary share had been converted into 30 new 3.33p. Ordinary shares.
• Huttonread took its name from the townland in which the farm at Blackchurch is situated.

FARMING

Farms, or more importantly, land, has always been an important of the asset base. Whether this was an attempt by some earlier family members to be seen as part of the landed gentry, as opposed to being merely 'trade', is not clear. But a substantial land bank was built up through individual holdings in Meelick (Portlaoise), Rathlease (Portarlington), Guileen (Stradbally) and at Quinnsboro at Blackchurch, Naas*. This last was the biggest landholding - expanded over time to almost 500 acres -which was bought by Claude Odlum just prior to the outbreak of WWII, with a view to securing food production in what might be a period of shortage.

In one sense, this could be seen as 'hobby' farming as opposed to a strictly commercial enterprise. The operations were indirectly managed by family members but the day-to-day operations were entrusted to a series of farm stewards and farmhands. This was not the most efficient way to manage the business and with an increasing focus on maximizing return on assets, most of the farms were sold off over time.

Without a doubt, the biggest coup was the sale of 125 acres of land at Quinnsboro, Naas at the height of the so-called Celtic Tiger for the extraordinary sum of £25 million - the equivalent of €200,000 per acre. All that remains of the once-sizeable land holdings are 355 acres at Quinnsboro and a further 40 hectares in Meelick, Portlaoise.

Jeremy Odlum pictured in his combine harvester at Blackchurch - 2006. Source PM Photography

* For some reason, only the farms at Guileen and Blackchurch were included in the list of assets held on 9 January 1952, prior to the formation of W.P.& R.O. Holdings. Guileen was valued at £685/13/0 and Quinnsboro at £20,908/17/11.